Cogniti

M000309290

Michael Neenan clearly and accessibly introduces the 30 Distinctive Features of cognitive behavioural coaching (CBC), an approach which applies the principles of CBT to coaching.

Cognitive Behavioural Coaching: Distinctive Features sets out the key theoretical and practical features of CBT and discusses how they integrate into the generic model of coaching. The book covers the four key elements in developing a coaching relationship, provides psychological and practical problem-solving models, shows how to deal with stuck points in coaching and identifies which individuals are unsuitable for CBC. As well as providing research evidence to support the effectiveness of CBC, the book demonstrates the smooth transition of CBT into CBC, and coach–coachee dialogues are interspersed throughout the text to show CBC in action.

Cognitive Behavioural Coaching: Distinctive Features will be particularly useful to CBT therapists interested in adding coaching to their practice. It will also appeal to coaches in practice and in training and other professionals in coaching roles seeking an effective and straightforward coaching model.

Michael Neenan is Associate Director of the Centre for Coaching and Centre for Stress Management, Blackheath, London. He is the author of *Developing Resilience: A Cognitive-Behavioural Approach* (second edition, Routledge).

Coaching Distinctive Features
Series Editor: Windy Dryden

Leading practitioners and theorists of coaching approaches write simply and briefly on what constitutes the main features of their particular approach. Each book highlights 30 main features, divided between theoretical and practical points. Written in a straightforward and accessible style, they can be understood by both those steeped in the coaching tradition and by those outside that tradition. The series editor is Windy Dryden.

Titles in the series:

Rational Emotive Behavioural Coaching by Windy Dryden

Cognitive Behavioural Coaching by Michael Neenan

For further information about this series please visit
www.routledge.com/Coaching-Distinctive-Features/book-series/CDF

Cognitive Behavioural Coaching

Distinctive Features

Michael Neenan

Routledge
Taylor & Francis Group

LONDON AND NEW YORK

First published 2018
by Routledge
2 Park Square, Milton Park, Abingdon, Oxon OX14 4RN

and by Routledge
711 Third Avenue, New York, NY 10017

Routledge is an imprint of the Taylor & Francis Group, an informa business

British Library Cataloguing in Publication Data
A catalogue record for this book is available from the British Library

Library of Congress Cataloging in Publication Data
Names: Neenan, Michael, author.
Title: Cognitive behavioural coaching / Michael Neenan.
Description: Abingdon, Oxon ; New York, NY : Routledge, 2018. | Series:
    Coaching distinctive features | Includes bibliographical references.
Identifiers: LCCN 2017047604 (print) | LCCN 2017055170 (ebook) | ISBN
    9781351188555 (Master e-book) | ISBN 9780815393429 (hardback) |
    ISBN 9780815393436 (pbk.)
Subjects: LCSH: Personal coaching. | Cognitive therapy.
Classification: LCC BF637.P36 (ebook) | LCC BF637.P36 N43 2018 (print) |
    DDC 158/.9—dc23
LC record available at https://lccn.loc.gov/2017047604

ISBN: 978-0-8153-9342-9 (hbk)
ISBN: 978-0-8153-9343-6 (pbk)
ISBN: 978-1-351-18855-5 (ebk)

Typeset in Times New Roman
by Swales & Willis Ltd, Exeter, Devon, UK

Contents

Tables

Introduction

From CBT to CBC

Coaching has been used in the business world for several decades for improving performance and developing talent. In recent years, the psychological theory and practice of particular therapeutic approaches have been adapted for use in coaching such as behavioural, cognitive behavioural, existential, solution focused, gestalt, person-centred and psychodynamic. A definition of coaching psychology is 'for enhancing well-being and performance in personal life and work domains underpinned by models of coaching grounded in established adult and child learning or psychological approaches' (quoted in Palmer and Whybrow, 2007: 3). A psychological approach to coaching helps individuals to: develop greater self-understanding; pinpoint and tackle psychological blocks to change; and improve their self-regulatory skills which increase the likelihood of goal achievement. Landsberg (2015) suggests that coaches are T-shaped: the crossbar of the T is the broad range of techniques used from diverse sources; the vertical bar of the T is the coach's preferred school of psychology. The vertical bar used in this book on coaching is cognitive behavioural psychology.

Cognitive behavioural coaching (CBC) derives from the work of two leading cognitive behavioural theorists, researchers and therapists: Aaron Beck, the founder of cognitive therapy (CT), and the late Albert Ellis who developed rational emotive behaviour therapy (REBT). These two approaches come under the umbrella term of cognitive behavioural therapy (CBT). CBT focuses on individuals' cognitive appraisals of events in order to understand their emotional and behavioural reactions to these events. Where a person might say 'The situation made me so angry', the cognitive behavioural therapist would ask, 'What was going through your mind in that situation that led to you being so angry?' in order to reveal the coachee's anger-producing thoughts: 'I was treated disrespectfully at the meeting: my opinion wasn't asked for as if it was valueless.' CBT is the first line treatment for a range of clinical disorders and 'is a psychological therapy with a most solid and wide evidence base for efficacy [it works well in research trials] and effectiveness [and in clinical practice]' (Kennerley et al., 2017: 20).

However, does the success of CBT in treating clinical disorders translate into similar success in coaching with individuals focused on personal and professional development? Since 2001, researchers have been building up an evidence base for CBC using qualitative, quantitative and single-case design studies (Neenan and Palmer, 2012). CBC has been shown to enhance, for example, goal-striving, well-being, hope, resilience, sales performance, emotional management and reduces self-handicapping thoughts, feelings and behaviours that interfere with performance and goal achievement. A definition of CBC is helping individuals to develop their capabilities in the areas they nominate with a particular focus on the beliefs, behaviours and emotions that help or hinder this development. For example, a technical specialist, now promoted to a management position, is apprehensive about their new role ('I'm not a natural people person type') and wants to learn people management skills. CBC offers different types of coaching:

- Life coaching – teaching people skills and attitudes to help them become self-empowered to achieve their goals, including workplace ones (Neenan and Dryden, 2014).
- Skills coaching – learning new skills and/or improving existing ones.
- Performance coaching – closing the gap between actual and desired performance.
- Resilience coaching – developing a resilience improvement plan (RIP), i.e. how to make yourself more resilient.
- Developmental coaching – a longer-term, open-ended approach which usually focuses on fundamental personal and professional issues.

CBC has many of the characteristics associated with the generic model of coaching: staying mainly in the present (information from the past may be collected to clarify the coachee's current concerns); setting goals; devising action plans; improving coachees' self-control strategies to keep them goal-focused; monitoring progress; teaching problem-solving skills; dealing with blocks to change. Therefore, CBC as a specialism and the generic model of coaching have a very good fit 'and is why the cognitive behavioural approach is fundamental to coaching' (Grant, 2012: xv).

The essential difference between therapy and coaching is usually stated as: the former focuses on disturbance and dysfunction while the latter seeks to unlock potential, improve performance, enhance well-being and deliver results. This is an unjust and inaccurate account of this difference. When a client comes to therapy for help with their panic attacks or obsessive compulsive disorder they are seeking results (overcoming the problem) which will lead to enhanced well-being, improved performance in their personal and/or professional life and release more of their potential previously inhibited by the problem. Indeed, from a CBT perspective, when clients are gaining in confidence as a self-therapist (i.e. independent problem solver), the therapist conceptualizes their role more as a coach supporting their clients' self-directed learning. Promoting coaching does not have to be done in a way that diminishes what therapy has to offer.

I believe there are more similarities than dissimilarities between the two approaches. Many of the difficulties people bring to therapy are the same as in coaching, such as: low self-esteem, perfectionism, performance anxiety, coping with uncertainty, feeling like a fraud, interpersonal difficulties, fear of failure, fear of being seen as weak or not in control, being bullied, procrastination, and anger. As one of my colleagues who moved into coaching from therapy commented: 'It's mostly the same old stuff but a different language is used to deal with it [e.g. developmental opportunities instead of weaknesses or problems].'

Sometimes a coachee will mask their problem in language designed to create the impression that there isn't a problem because, in their mind, emotional problems are equated with weakness. So it's presented as an emotion-free, practical or technical issue, for example, 'I just want to focus on a couple of factors that might result in delivering a suboptimal performance' or 'Occasionally I'm gripped by granularity [level of detail]'. In these two examples, the investigation of each coachee's concerns revealed that they had the same fear (and a widespread one): being exposed as incompetent was their core belief and anxiety was the emotion they struggled with; they felt ashamed about feeling anxious.

When I see individuals in therapy and coaching with the same problem such as fear of public speaking (FPS), there is nothing fundamentally different in my approach to helping them as they have similar patterns of thoughts, feelings and behaviours relating to their FPS. I use a common language for both groups such as 'helpful/unhelpful thoughts' and 'productive/unproductive behaviours'. I no longer use terms like 'irrational thinking' or 'dysfunctional behaviour' with my therapy clients.

Of course, therapy is the right place for the severely distressed, but no one is immune to experiencing emotional problems. Some research studies 'have found that between 25 and 50 per cent of those seeking coaching have clinically significant levels of anxiety, stress or depression' (Grant, 2009: 97) and these emotional problems are likely to interfere in coaching (Dryden, 2011). With their understanding and treatment of psychological disorders, cognitive behavioural therapists who have moved into coaching after a period of transitional training (Sperry, 2004) would be more likely than coaches without a background in mental health to recognize when it would be appropriate to refer a coachee for therapy. Before a referral is considered, cognitive behavioural coaches would attempt to ameliorate these emotional problems in order to refocus coachees' attention on achieving their goals; in the majority of cases a referral wouldn't be necessary. Thus, CBC has two main elements: goal achievement and the removal, if they emerge, of psychological blocks that impede goal-striving. In Part I, we look at cognitive behavioural theory which underpins CBC.

Part I

COGNITIVE BEHAVIOURAL THEORY

1

Eliciting meaning

'At the very heart of the C[B]T model is the view that the human mind is not a passive receptacle of environmental and biological influences and sensations, but rather that individuals are actively involved in constructing their reality' (Clark, 1995: 156). In order to understand a person's emotional response to particular life events, it's important to discover the meaning they attach to these events: their subjective construction of reality. For example, a person whose partner has left them believes they cannot be happy or cope on their own and becomes depressed; another person whose partner has departed feels relieved as they believe they have been freed from a 'stifling relationship'; a third person feels guilty as they view their bad behaviour as the reason for their partner's departure – the same event for each person, but not the same emotional reaction to it as each reaction is mediated by the person's view of the event. In order to change the way we feel about events we need to change the way we think about them. Meaning isn't static but changes over time, that is, your viewpoint alters.

This conceptual cornerstone of cognitive behavioural therapy (CBT) derives from ancient Stoic philosophers such as Epictetus and Marcus Aurelius and their views on mental control. That is to say, our thoughts and beliefs are within our control whereas many things that happen to us in life are outside of our control; therefore, we can choose how we respond to events. Events themselves do not cause or dictate our reactions, for example, losing your job in a recession is outside of your control but losing your self-respect as well is a judgement *you* have made about being jobless (for a fascinating discussion on the links between Stoic philosophy and CBT, see Robertson [2010]. I've met executives who proudly showed me their copies of

3

Marcus Aurelius's *Meditations* and Epictetus's *Handbook* which they said taught them how to develop the inner stability to cope with the unrelenting pressures of the workplace).

Modern CBT doesn't argue that a person's emotional problems are simply created in their head but that the impact of adverse events (e.g. being burgled) can be greatly exacerbated by the person's unhelpful thoughts and beliefs that interfere with their ability to cope constructively with such events (e.g. 'I can never ever feel safe again in my own home no matter how many locks I put on the doors and windows'). Clients are helped to develop adaptive viewpoints in order to tackle their problems (e.g. 'If I keep things in perspective, I know that the increased security measures will help to keep me safe in my home and my mind, but I realize and accept, without liking it, that there can be no guarantee I won't be burgled again').

Developing an alternative viewpoint underscores the CBT principle that there is *always* more than one way of seeing things, no matter how unpleasant these things are. Even in the unspeakable horrors of Auschwitz, Viktor Frankl, a famous psychiatrist, observed that 'everything can be taken from a man but one thing: the last of the human freedoms – to choose one's attitude in any given set of circumstances, to choose one's own way' (1946/1985: 86). Coutu (2003) states that Frankl's theory is the basis for much of the resilience coaching in the business world.

2

Distorted information processing

Cognitive theory is based on an information-processing model 'which posits that during psychological distress a person's thinking becomes more rigid and distorted, judgements become overgeneralized and absolute, and the person's basic beliefs about the self and the world become fixed' (Weishaar, 1996: 188). In a calmer frame of mind, the person is likely to check their impressions and appraisals of events in order to obtain clear and accurate information. However, everyone engages in distorted information professing such as jumping to conclusions or mind-reading (see below) but these distortions 'only become a problem when the bias is chronic or too extreme' (Kennerley et al., 2017: 193).

When emotionally upset the person will usually distort incoming information by introducing a consistently negative bias into their thinking, for example, they are upset when not invited to a friend's party because they interpret the lack of an invitation to mean that they are an unlikeable person. Instead of ascertaining the reasons for not being invited, or keeping an open mind about it, the person dwells on their supposed unlikeability, lowering their mood in the process.

Distorted thinking underlies psychological problems. These distortions usually stem from deeper negative beliefs that are activated during emotional distress, for instance, a person experiencing depression after the break-up of their relationship insists 'I'll always be alone' (fortune-telling) because they believe they are unattractive (core belief). Common information-processing errors or biases found in emotional distress include the following.

- All or nothing thinking: situations and individuals are viewed in either/or terms, e.g. 'Either you're a success or failure in life. It's as simple as that'.
- Emotional reasoning: believing that feelings are facts, e.g. 'I feel repulsive, so it must be true'. 'I feel repulsive' is actually a belief ('I believe I'm repulsive'), not a feeling, and therefore is subject to examination like any other belief.
- Jumping to conclusions: judgements are rushed rather than considered, e.g. a client says 15 minutes into the first session: 'This isn't going to work as I don't feel any better'.
- Mind-reading: discerning the thoughts of others without any accompanying evidence to support such claims, e.g. 'My boss didn't smile at me this morning, so that means she's unhappy with my work' (she praised their work previously without smiling at them).
- Labelling: attaching global negative labels to oneself, others or the world, e.g. 'I didn't understand what he said, unlike others in the group, so this must mean I'm stupid' (they're also mind-reading in assuming that everyone else in the group understood what was said).

Teaching clients how to identify and correct these errors or biases in their thinking facilitates the return of information processing that is more evidence-based and balanced (non-absolute). In the example above, the person discovers that their friend had invited them but 'my mother forgot to pass on the message. If I hadn't got so upset, then I wouldn't have jumped to conclusions'. If they hadn't been invited and it was expected that they would be, then they need to contact their friend to find out why they have been excluded from the invitation list. Even if their friend deliberately excluded them, this does not mean they are an unlikeable person, but a person not immune to their friendships ending and having to learn to adapt to this unwelcome reality.

3

Levels of thought

There are three levels to consider.

1. *Negative automatic thoughts* (NATs) are situation-specific and involuntarily 'pop into' a person's mind when they are experiencing psychological difficulties. They appear plausible to them and are difficult to turn off. NATs often lie outside of immediate awareness but can be quickly brought to the client's attention by asking, 'What was going through your mind at that moment when you got to the meeting late?' (Client's reply: 'I'm always late. I'm undisciplined, sloppy. My colleagues will look down on me'). NATs can be triggered by external and/or internal events (e.g. pounding heart: 'I'm having a heart attack. Oh God! I'm going to die').

NATs can also occur as images, for example, a person sees himself 'dying of embarrassment' if he makes a faux pas as best man at his friend's wedding. Clients are usually more aware of how they feel than of the thoughts that prompted the feeling. In coaching as in therapy, NATs are usually the starting point for investigation. The alternative thoughts to NATs are not PATs (positive automatic thoughts) as they can be equally distorted (e.g. 'Once the problem is gone, it won't reoccur'), but thoughts based on reason and evidence that remove cognitive distortions from the person's view of events.

2. *Underlying assumptions* (e.g. 'If I impress others, then I should get ahead in life') and *rules* (e.g. 'I should not let people down') guide behaviour and set standards. These assumptions and rules are often unarticulated and can be difficult for clients to detect, unlike NATs. Underlying assumptions are usually identified by their 'if . . . then' or 'unless . . . then' construction, and rules are usually expressed in

7

'must' and 'should' statements. These assumptions and rules are the means by which individuals hope to avoid coming 'face-to-face' with their negative core beliefs (e.g. 'I'm incompetent'). The 'truth' of these core beliefs is not usually questioned and, therefore, assumptions and rules serve to maintain and strengthen them.

Trouble looms for the person when their behaviour is not what it should be, standards are not met or rules are violated – 'trouble' is the activation of the negative core belief from its dormant state. Beck et al. (1985) suggest that unhelpful assumptions often focus on three major issues: acceptance (e.g. 'I'm nothing unless I'm loved'); competence (e.g. 'I am what I accomplish'); and control (e.g. 'I can't ask for help'). Worries about not being seen to be in control of oneself or events, acting incompetently or losing the respect/approval of colleagues are common themes in coaching. Assumptions and rules are cross-situational and are also known as intermediate beliefs because they lie between NATs and core beliefs (J. S. Beck, 2011).

3. *Core beliefs* are the deepest level of thought. Negative core beliefs are overgeneralized and unconditional (e.g. 'I'm hopeless'). They are usually formed through earlier learning experiences and lie dormant until activated by relevant life events. For example, the person believes they're worthless without a partner: they're anxious when the present relationship goes through turbulent times ('Is this the end?') and depressed if it does end thereby confirming their core belief. Once activated, negative core beliefs process information in a biased way that confirms them and disconfirms contradictory information (e.g. 'I can't learn to live on my own for a while and be more independent. I must find someone else'). Core beliefs can be about the self (e.g. 'I'm unloveable'), others (e.g. 'I can't trust anyone'), and/or the world (e.g. 'Everything is against me'). Once the distress has passed (e.g. they're relieved when they find a new partner), negative core beliefs become deactivated or return to their latent state and a more positive outlook is re-established.

Core beliefs are usually the targets of change in longstanding problems. Core beliefs can be modified indirectly by targeting NATs as they are situation-specific expressions of core beliefs.

This indirect targeting also helps to reactivate quiescent positive core beliefs ('I'm likeable') which became inactive due to the dominance of the negative beliefs. Dobson and Dobson (2009) suggest that it's quite likely that negative core beliefs change gradually without directly modifying them if clients continue to think and act differently over the longer term. In coaching, negative core beliefs are targeted for change if required; for example, a highly successful executive takes little pleasure in their achievements 'because, at bottom, I'm a fraud' and wants to stop seeing themself in this way.

How do these three levels interact? A person feels depressed when they fail to get a first in their university exams. Their dormant core belief, 'I'm a failure', is activated by their inability to live up to their rigid rule that they must meet the high expectations placed on them by others and their mind is flooded with NATs: 'I can't show my face at university. Run away and hide. The whole university is laughing at me. I've lost the respect of my friends.'

4

Thoughts, feelings, behaviour, physiology and the situation are interconnected

In the cognitive model, uncovering the meaning (thoughts and beliefs) that people attach to events is crucial for understanding their emotional and behavioural reactions to events. However, cognition in cognitive behavioural therapy (CBT) is not viewed in isolation from other response systems within the person but recognizes its interaction with behaviour, physiology and emotions. These systems interact within the wider context of a person's environment such as having noisy neighbours or living in a high crime area. Each one of these elements is capable of influencing the others in an interactive cycle. Seeing the linkages between these five areas of a person's experience can help them to understand better their present difficulties. For example, they've lost their job (situation) and see themself as worthless (belief), feel depressed (emotion), withdraw from social activity (behaviour) and complain of constant tiredness (physiology).

A change in one of these five areas, such as a return to being sociable, produces positive change in the other four: they look for another job (situation); see themself again as a person of worth (belief); their depressed mood lifts (emotion); and they start to feel re-energized (physiology). A five-areas model used in cognitive behavioural coaching (CBC) is SPACE (Edgerton and Palmer, 2005): Social context, Physiology, Action, Cognitions and Emotions (see Chapter 13).

The usual entry point to help a person understand this interactive process is by identifying their situation-specific negative automatic thoughts (NATs): 'Do you know what you were thinking [belief] while waiting for the train [situation] that made you feel so jittery [physiology] and anxious [emotion] that you paced up and down on the platform [behaviour]?' Any of these five elements can be the entry point to link the other four, such as a coachee saying they always develop a tight stomach (physiology) before meetings with their boss. Teaching this interactive process does not undermine a core proposition in CBT: that cognitive change is central to the human change process (Clark and Steer, 1996).

5

A continuum of emotional reactions

There is continuity between 'normal' emotional reactions to life events and excessive or extreme emotional reactions. As Weisharr and Beck (1986: 65) explain:

> *The cognitive content of syndromes (e.g. anxiety disorders, depression) have the same theme (e.g. danger or loss, respectively) as found in 'normal' experience, but cognitive distortions are extreme and, consequently, so are affect [emotion] and behaviour.*

For example, a person looking over their life might experience sadness at the wasted opportunities but knows that new ones lie ahead; however, their sadness may intensify and become a prolonged depression if they see such wasted opportunities as the *whole* story of their life. With physiological reactions (e.g. heart pounding, sweating, trembling), they would be the same for a person who believes they are about to be attacked (physical threat) as for a person who fears making mistakes in front of others (psychosocial threat).

Normal and exaggerated emotional reactions to events are characterized, respectively, by what Beck et al. (1979) call 'mature' (flexible) and 'primitive' (absolute) thinking. For example, a mature response to being disliked might be that 'you can't please everyone' whereas a primitive response might conclude that 'I'm thoroughly unlikeable' because some people don't like them. Explaining to clients this continuum of emotional reactions to life events helps to remove some of the stigma from emotional distress and thereby normalizes it, that is, everyone goes up and down the continuum. There is no qualitative difference, as some argue, between emotions in therapy (disturbed) and in coaching (mild, only troublesome). Anyone who engages in extreme thinking (e.g. 'I can't stand it when things go wrong!') is likely to experience extreme emotions (e.g. intense anger) and find themselves at the extreme end of the continuum.

6

Emotions have a specific cognitive content

This means there are specific themes running through particular emotions. For example, devaluation or loss in depression, danger or threat in anxiety, situationally specific danger in phobia, transgression of personal rules and standards in anger, moral lapse in guilt, perceived deficiencies revealed to others in shame, and expansion in happiness. These themes are tied to Beck's (1976) concept of the 'personal domain', that is, anything that the person considers important in their life. The nature of 'a person's emotional response – or emotional disturbance – depends on whether he perceives events as adding to, subtracting from, endangering, or impinging upon his domain' (Beck, 1976: 56). Some examples will help to explain this relationship:

- A person who prides themself on being a successful business-person becomes depressed when their company goes bust because they believe, 'My work is my life. Without my company, I'm nothing' (subtraction).
- A person becomes anxious that their sexual prowess will be ridiculed when they experience erectile dysfunction (endangerment).
- A person is delighted that they have been promoted as this is now another significant step in their career path (expansion).
- A person who enjoys peace and quiet in their life becomes very angry when their new next-door neighbour plays their music very loudly (impingement).

A person may experience different emotions with the same event on separate occasions depending on the event's relevance to their personal domain. For example, a person may feel anxious on Monday when the train is late as they will then be late for an important meeting, and this might appear to others that they're trying to impress that they're unpunctual with its connotations of being undisciplined (endangerment); angry on Tuesday when the train is late as this means more people will board it at their station thereby restricting their personal space on the train (impingement).

7

Cognitive vulnerability

Vulnerability can be defined as an 'endogenous [internal] stable characteristic that remains latent until activated by a precipitating event' (Clark and Beck, 2010: 102). An event that may trigger vulnerability in one person (e.g. low mood after receiving a highly critical performance appraisal) is viewed with equanimity by another (e.g. 'I'll just have to do better next time'). Two broad personality types who would be at risk for depression or anxiety are sociotropy and autonomy:

> *The sociotropic personality orientation places a high value on having close interpersonal relations, with a strong emphasis on being loved and valued by others. On the other hand, the autonomous personality orientation reflects a high investment in personal independence, [need for control], achievement and freedom of choice.*
>
> *(Clark and Steer, 1996: 81)*

A typical sociotropic belief is 'I must be loved in order to be happy' and a typical autonomous belief is 'I must be a success in order to be worthwhile' (Beck, 1987).

Anxiety can occur if, for example, there is a perceived threat to a close relationship or the danger of a career setback; if this threat or danger is realized, then depression is likely to ensue. The match between a person's specific vulnerability (e.g. no close friends means they are unlikeable) and a significant life event that reflects this predisposition (e.g. their closest friend won't speak to them any more) is likened by Beck (1987) to a key fitting into a lock to open the door to depression. Scott (2009) points out that there are varying degrees of vulnerability, so a number of adverse life events may need to occur rather than just one before depression descends. For example, for an autonomous person, failing to achieve an important business goal and becoming ill and dependent on others.

8

Our thoughts and beliefs are both knowable and accessible

Between an external stimulus (e.g. being criticized) and an emotional response to it (e.g. anger) lie a person's thoughts about this event. Eliciting these thoughts helps the person to understand why they reacted to the event in the way that they did. Beck calls this 'tapping the internal communications' and states that clients can be trained 'to focus on their introspections [examining one's thoughts] in various situations. The person can then observe that a thought links the external stimulus with the emotional response' (1976: 27). Asking a client such questions as 'What was going through your mind at that moment?' or 'What were you thinking about in that situation?' can help to turn their attention inwards rather than remain focused on the external event which they might assume 'caused' their emotional reaction.

In the above example, the person is able to uncover their thoughts which contributed to their anger: 'How dare he criticize me! I've done nothing wrong to deserve this. He's a bastard!' Helping a client to detect, examine and change their disturbance-producing thoughts means that this process can be accomplished 'within the scope of his own awareness' (Beck, 1976: 3) rather than such thoughts remaining inaccessible to them. This process of cognitive change within the scope of a person's awareness enables them to eventually become their own therapist or coach, i.e. an independent problem solver. The lifelong challenge is to keep this awareness psychologically healthy, that is, based on open-mindedness in addressing concerns or pursuing goals, not closed-mindedness that perpetuates problems. As the saying goes, the mind, like a parachute, works best when it's open.

A client might experience an emotional response without an obvious external stimulus to trigger it; in this case, the client needs to search for an internal stimulus such as an image (e.g. seeing themself stammering in front of an audience) or a memory (e.g. being shouted at by a schoolteacher) in order to understand why their feeling seemed to 'come out of the blue'.

In Chapter 3, I described three levels of cognition (negative automatic thoughts [NATs], assumptions/rules, and core beliefs) in understanding emotional disorders. These levels usually correspond with the degree of difficulty in gaining access to them. Surface thoughts (NATs) are usually on the fringe of awareness, though they can be quickly brought to the front of the client's mind by asking the questions already mentioned above. Underlying assumptions/rules and core beliefs often remain unarticulated and, therefore, can be more difficult to gain access to. Linking NATs to underlying (intermediate and core) beliefs is achieved by asking the client to probe for the logical implications of each NAT (e.g. 'If it's true that you cry easily, what does that mean to you?') until important rules (e.g. 'I should always be strong and never reveal any vulnerabilities') and core beliefs (e.g. 'I'm weak') are uncovered (see Chapter 24). Peeling away layers of personal meaning makes explicit what was previously implicit.

9

Maintenance of problems

Cognitive behavioural therapy (CBT) 'considers *current* cognitive functioning crucial to the maintenance and persistence of psychological disturbance' (Clark, 1995: 158; emphasis in original). By staying mainly in the present, the client focuses on modifying their current unhelpful thoughts (e.g. 'I can't be happy without him'), assumptions (e.g. 'If he's abandoned me, then no one else will ever want me') and core beliefs (e.g. 'I'm unloveable') in order to ameliorate their emotional distress. Historical factors (e.g. parental neglect, bullied at school, severe acne during adolescence) that contributed to the person's current problems (e.g. low self-esteem) cannot be modified; current beliefs and behaviours that maintain these problems can be. While many people might believe that present-day progress can only be achieved when the putative childhood origins (root causes) of their problems have been uncovered and addressed,

> decades of research on cognitive-behavior, behavioral, and interpersonal therapies demonstrate that although tracing the presumed early causes of people's difficulties can sometimes offer a helpful perspective on current problems, it is rarely a necessary ingredient for improvement. Indeed, these effective treatments focus largely on the here and now.
>
> *(Arkowitz and Lilienfeld, 2017: 211)*

With a new perspective, the past can be psychologically restructured: 'I now realize that it wasn't my fault that my father left when I was five – I supposedly drove him out as my mother always claimed. She was blaming me for the failure of the marriage.'

Sometimes a coachee will complain, for example, of a bullying boss, which triggers unpleasant memories of being bullied at school and feeling as helpless then as they do now. While the coachee might want to dwell on being bullied at school, the main focus in coaching would be on learning attitudes and skills to assertively challenge their boss about his or her behaviour. The coachee's active stance towards the boss is in stark and welcome contrast to their feelings of helplessness at school when the bully struck.

Behaviour plays a very important role in maintaining problems as individuals act in ways that support their unhelpful beliefs – you act as you think. For example, a person buys some self-assembly furniture; they don't immediately understand the instructions (as they should do) and the pieces don't fit together immediately (as they should do) when the person makes a start on trying to assemble them. They stare helplessly at the pieces lying on the floor and conclude: 'I'll never be able to assemble all this crap!' Angry at themself for their perceived DIY uselessness, they throw all the pieces into the dustbin. They could have persevered, asked a friend with some DIY skills to show them how to do it, or paid a handyman to assemble it for them or teach them to do it for themself. A low tolerance for experiencing frustration stopped them from pursuing the first option and embarrassment the other two. In summary, cognitive and behaviour change are both important (hence CBT).

10

A strong commitment to scientific empiricism

This means seeking scientific evidence for cognitive behavioural theory and the effectiveness of its clinical interventions (Clark and Beck, 2010). Scientific empiricism is not only a method but also a mindset – the willingness to abandon key cognitive behavioural therapy (CBT) tenets if not supported by research evidence. Therapists are encouraged to adopt the stance of a scientist-practitioner by drawing on research evidence to inform their clinical practice as well as evaluating the effectiveness of their own practice; clients are also encouraged to take an empirical stance by subjecting their problematic thoughts and beliefs to examination and reality-testing in order to construct more helpful and accurate viewpoints.

In coaching, I frequently use the image of the workplace as a laboratory where thoughts and beliefs can be tested. For example, an executive chairing a meeting with her clients was anxious about 'spontaneity breaking out' (i.e. her clients not sticking to the prepared agenda) as her hard-worked-on, well-prepared answers might seem insufficient to them and 'I'm not sure how well I'll be able to think on my feet'. At the next meeting with them, she didn't try to dampen down the spontaneity and was surprised how well her off-the-cuff contributions were received and how quickly her anxiety abated. It's one thing to explain to clients in the session, whether in therapy or coaching, the possible benefits of new ways of acting but putting it to the test in the actual situations usually deepens and quickens the process of change.

The image CBT wants to convey is that of two scientists working together to define problems, formulate and test hypotheses about them and find problem-solving options. Beck et al. (1979) call this working together as two scientists or co-investigators 'collaborative empiricism'. Working as co-investigators into problem solving guards against the possibility of the relationship becoming one of guru and disciple – this partnership in problem solving provides the success in therapy or coaching, not the unilateral actions of the therapist or coach. Also, working together disabuses clients of the notion that the therapist's or coach's job is to 'fix me' while they remain passive in the 'fixing' process.

Poor science can occur in this collaborative enterprise if the therapist or coach wants only to *confirm* their hypotheses about the client's problems (e.g. 'It's definitely an approval issue') and the client continually discounts the data that contradict their negative beliefs (e.g. 'Successes don't count, failures do; therefore, I'm a failure'). Developing and maintaining open-mindedness means that both parties speak from the collected data rather than from personal opinion or prejudice.

While the emphasis here is on empiricism – testing one's beliefs and assumptions in real-life settings in order to gather evidence to support, modify or discard them – reason is also used to help clients improve their critical thinking skills by looking at flaws and weaknesses in the arguments they use to support their self- and goal-defeating beliefs. Knowledge acquired through the application of reason and the collection of evidence helps to increase the chances of goal success.

Critics of CBT argue that science cannot answer all questions of importance about the human condition. There are other ways of knowing than just through science: literature, art, philosophy, our passionate interests and core values can bring insight and enlightenment into the private realm of our inner experiences. This kind of knowledge is what the philosopher Bryan Magee (2016: 115) calls 'knowledge from within'; scientific methods and discoveries which are open to all he calls 'knowledge from without': '. . . the most promising path towards an understanding of the nature of things lies partially within as well as partially without. In fact it seems self-evident' (Magee, 2016: 115). In my experience, not every CB therapist or coach would call themselves a 'strict empiricist' in the sense of being led in their practice only by research data (I would include myself in this group).

11

The law of parsimony

Cognitive behavioural therapy (CBT) follows the law of parsimony or Ockham's razor: 'If you can explain something adequately without introducing further complexity, then the simple explanation is the best explanation' (Warburton, 2007: 107). For example, a coachee complains of feeling angry when their boss gives them extra work (e.g. 'It's not fair! Because I finish my work first, I get punished for being efficient'). Understanding and moderating their anger will not usually be advanced by them attempting to pinpoint their boss's putative motives, developing a psychological profile of them, and/or repeatedly discussing the corporate culture. Helping them to see that they are not exempt from experiencing unfairness in the workplace (or anywhere else) and addressing their concerns to their boss may prove to be straightforward solutions to their anger problem.

When further complexity is necessary, explanations still follow the law of parsimony in 'specifying the simplest *sufficient* explanation for a stated purpose' (Naugle and Follette, 1998: 67; emphasis in original). The coachee's longstanding belief, 'I'm a phoney and will eventually be found out for what I really am', was revealed, which they found sufficient and satisfactory in explaining why they drive themself relentlessly to finish their work first to prove to their boss how efficient they are and thereby, in their mind, are able to keep pushing back the day of exposure as a fraud. Core beliefs like 'I'm a phoney' are both straightforward and fundamental in explaining the source (cognitive root causes) and maintenance of clients' problems.

Part II

COGNITIVE BEHAVIOURAL PRACTICE

12

The coaching relationship

The cognitive behavioural approach to coaching is explained to the coachee – a problem-solving partnership focused on producing an optimal outcome for the coachee – and the expected roles of both parties are outlined: the coach showing how the cognitive behavioural coaching (CBC) model can be applied to the coachee's concerns and the coachee carrying out their goal-related extra-session tasks. Of fundamental importance is the coachee taking responsibility for their thoughts, feelings and behaviours rather than blaming others for the way they think, feel and act. Not taking psychological responsibility is one of the major reasons CBC is ineffective for some coachees (see Chapter 30). Any comments, reservations or criticisms about this approach are sought from the coachee. The number of sessions is negotiated and can be extended if required (unless the number of sessions has been fixed in advance).

It's important not to assume that the coachee is at the starting line, ready to go, for example, 'I think this is the approach for me but I'm not yet decided' as this indicates they want more discussion about how CBC could help them before they commit themself to it. The coach needs to keep in step with the coachee's degree of readiness to change (e.g. ambivalent, apprehensive) and address their concerns ('Everything we do is based on agreement, not coercion') in order to nudge them towards the starting line. Dealing with ambivalence – mixed feelings about changing or staying with the status quo – is a frequent task for both therapists and coaches. One method of handling ambivalence is motivational interviewing (Miller and Rollnick, 2013) whereby the coach helps the coachee to strengthen their intrinsic motivation for change by seeing more benefits in changing than staying the same. Through this process, the coachee becomes the agent of change rather than being led along by the coach.

Furnham (2012) says, based on attempts by academics to calculate the percentage contribution of four key factors that lead to a successful outcome in coaching or therapy, that readiness to change accounts for 40% of the effectiveness of coaching (the other three factors are explained below). When the coachee is ready to commit to change, the coach discusses with them the likely hard work ahead. An uncompromising definition of personal responsibility for goal success is provided by Grieger (2017: 19; emphasis in original): 'Responsibility is a **belief** in which one holds oneself **100% responsible** for honoring one's promises and commitments and producing intended results, no matter how hard it may be'. Though this definition may sound extreme to some coachees, at least it's a starting point for discussing the meaning of true commitment to change.

Coachees can be asked if they have any preferences about how the coaching relationship is conducted in order to tailor it to these requirements, for instance, 'I want to think out loud about this issue I'm struggling with and I want you to provide some ideas, make comments as we go along so I can get a clearer picture of what I need to do to resolve this issue'. Coachees' relationship preferences need to be honoured and monitored as some of these preferences could prove detrimental to achieving success in coaching. In the above example, the coachee rejects all the coach's comments and ideas as they actually want to resolve the issue within the scope of their own constricted thinking, but they don't have the metacognitive awareness (thinking about their own thinking) to see how constricted it is. The coach offers this viewpoint to the coachee who reluctantly agrees and starts to consider some of the coach's ideas to widen their problem-solving perspective. The relationship accounts for roughly 30% towards a successful outcome (Norcross, 2002) but it's the coachee's view of the relationship, not the coach's, that's the important factor, so regular feedback from the coachee is required to keep it in good running order.

The other two factors in effective coaching are the coach instilling in the coachee expectations of success (15%) and the application of their particular theory (e.g. cognitive behavioural, existential, psychodynamic) to guide change (15%). If the coachee is not persuaded by the CBC approach, then coaching should be ended rather than the coach trying to persuade the coachee to change their mind in order for the coach to avoid judging themself as incompetent. These four factors Furnham observes (2012: 82) 'apply (roughly) equally to all forms of counseling, therapy, coaching or whatever the help is called'.

Honouring coachees' relationship preferences suggests a high degree of adaptability on the coach's part which, in my experience of supervising coaches and therapists, is often overestimated. Listening to digital voice recordings (DVRs) of sessions (see Chapter 28), the coach can be embarrassed and surprised by how quickly they revert to their normal interpersonal style and the coachees' preferences are forgotten. If coaches want to increase their interpersonal adaptiveness, then they need to tolerate the discomfort of acting in seemingly unnatural ways, for example, the fast-paced, impatient coach meets a slow, reflective responder to their questions and they need to learn to accept the inevitable silences that follow (see Chapter 22).

There are no private agendas in CBC: the coach shares their ideas with the coachee in order to underline the importance of collaborative empiricism (discussed in Chapter 10), that is, ideas are assumptions which need to be revealed, examined and tested, not treated as facts. Having pointed this out to the coachee, it's important that the coach acts non-defensively when their ideas are challenged or questioned. It's likely that both coach and coachee will have thoughts, behaviours and emotions that will interfere with the coaching process. For example, the coachee complains of slow progress, 'You're not really helping me', and the coach responds irritably: 'I've explained to you already that the between sessions tasks are crucial in achieving your goals and need to be carried out in a consistent, determined way, not the half-hearted, quickly giving-up approach which you keep employing, I'm sad to say.'

Impasses or ruptures in the coaching relationship can be resolved through what Safran and Muran (2000) call 'metacommunication' – the coach and coachee stepping outside of the strained relationship in order to comment upon it in a non-blaming spirit of collaborative inquiry. For example, the coachee agrees to find the time each week to carry out the tasks in a non-rushed, methodical way and the coach agrees to stop acting like a taskmaster. The coach carries the main responsibility for initiating and maintaining the meta-communication process.

Assessment and case conceptualization

Once cognitive behavioural coaching (CBC) has been explained and informed consent given to proceed, an initial and usually brief CBC assessment is carried out which focuses on the coachee's current concerns, the context in which they arise, what they wish to achieve in coaching and any additional information they would like to add to the assessment. This information is distilled into a brief case conceptualization. The reason it's brief is because there is no assumption that psychological blocks will interfere with the coachee's focus on goal achievement and/or carrying out extra-session tasks; if these blocks appear, a more detailed conceptualization may be developed. The coachee's strengths are also listed to aid goal-striving and remind them of past problem-solving successes and career achievements.

It's important to distinguish between problems and psychological blocks: solving the former can be a relatively straightforward process through the coachee's adoption of CBC's experimental outlook (i.e. trying out different problem-solving options), whereas the latter are usually ingrained beliefs and behaviours that can be hard to change and the coachee is ambivalent about changing them. For example, an executive was blocked from further advancement in his company until they moderated their abrasive interpersonal style. The coachee said that abrasiveness was part of their driven personality to succeed, it made others fear them (which the coachee saw as respect) and work harder than they would do for 'a soft boss'. The coachee railed against their company for 'blackmailing me' but eventually decided that moderating their interpersonal style was the preferred and pragmatic goal-related choice.

To return to the brief assessment, the coachee's (Sarah's) goal was to finish a report within a specified period but she kept putting off starting it. The SPACE model (Edgerton and Palmer, 2005) was used to understand her difficulties. This model is often used 'in brief coaching . . . and can serve as a simple case conceptualisation' (Palmer and Szymanska, 2007: 89). The model was written down on a flipchart:

> **S**ocial context: 'I make time at work to start the report then I let other tasks get in the way and therefore don't get on with it. The deadline for it to be completed is fast approaching.'
>
> **P**hysiology: 'I feel tight and tense when I think about starting the report.'
>
> **A**ction: 'I'll go get a coffee just before I start but by the time I get back to my desk I've thought of something else to do.'
>
> **C**ognitions: 'I've got this idea, as silly as it may seem, that the report has got to be written in one go and without any mistakes.'
>
> **E**motions: 'I feel anxious about not starting it as I'm falling behind, anxious about starting it as it won't be good enough and angry with myself for behaving like this.'

Other models can be used in brief coaching which combine assessment, goal-setting and practical problem solving within them such as PRACTICE (**P**roblem identification; **R**ealistic goals; **A**lternative solutions generated; **C**onsideration of consequences; **T**arget most feasible solution(s); **I**mplementation of **C**hosen solution(s); **E**valuation of outcome; Palmer and Szymanska, 2007) and ADAPT (see Chapter 21). A detailed case conceptualization is usually developed if there is no progress in coaching or it's clear from the outset that the coachee's problems are complex ones. If this is the case, there are three areas to cover.

1. *Obtaining more information*
   This involves asking the coachee (John) to provide several SPACE examples to determine how pervasive the problem is. Every example provided converged on the same fear: 'I might

not be able to answer a question to the satisfaction of the questioner and I'll be exposed as incompetent.' Certain situations at work, he said, contained the threat of exposure.

2. *Identifying key cognitive and behavioural maintaining processes*
Cognitive factors: 'If I know everything about my areas of responsibility then no one can catch me out' (assumption).

'If I can control the course of a conversation, then I won't be placed in a situation where I might be asked a totally unexpected question' (assumption).

'I must always make a good impression on my colleagues and superiors' (rule).

The associated behavioural strategy was to try and control situations to avoid being 'found out', i.e. not up to the job. For example:

- If John over-prepared then he could provide comprehensive answers to everyone's satisfaction but often he struggled to provide clear overviews of the projects he was working on, sometimes getting lost in detail and starting to ramble.
- John tried to control the flow of some conversations so he would be asked questions he knew he could answer well but, embarrassingly, sometimes provided answers to questions he wasn't asked because he wasn't following the *actual* flow of the conversation.
- John left only a couple of minutes or less at the end of team meetings in case he struggled with a question he wasn't expecting and could excuse himself by saying he had to rush off to another meeting and would give a full reply at the next team meeting (he said his team knew about his insecurities).

These cognitive and behavioural processes were counterproductive: the standards John set himself were too high, so he was anxious that he might fall below them and downhearted when he did. He said that no one, apart from his first boss, ever called him incompetent. He knew deep down he wasn't really incompetent but frequently struggled to convince himself of that when things went wrong.

3. *A longitudinal view*

This looks at how past factors have contributed to the coachee's current problems. The coachee said that his first boss, some years earlier, humiliated him at a meeting by calling him incompetent for giving a poor presentation: 'He said I didn't know my stuff and I wouldn't get very far in my career. I thought everyone around the table probably agreed with him.' This public rebuking served as an 'awful warning' of what could happen again if John wasn't a master of his material and he would need to work hard to create a favourable impression of himself in the eyes of others. From the assessment information, the case conceptualization was distilled (see Box 13.1).

Butler et al. (2008) advance three key principles which guide case conceptualization.

1. A conceptualization should be based on attempting to translate theory into practice, i.e. making sense of the coachee's problems within the cognitive behavioural model.
2. A conceptualization should be hypothetical: both coach and coachee are able to confirm, modify or discount the information used in developing one.
3. The conceptualization should be parsimonious (concise and clear). The more complex the conceptualization, the harder it will be to remember and use for both the coach and coachee.

Box 13.1 John's case conceptualization

Earlier experience

Felt humiliated when his first boss at a meeting publicly rebuked him for being incompetent in his project presentation. John took this rebuke to heart and believed he was incompetent (core belief) and must not be exposed as such again.

Cross-situational assumptions and rules (hoping to keep the core belief inactive)

'If I know everything about my areas of responsibility, then no one will be able to catch me out' (assumption)

'If I can control the course of a conversation, then I won't be placed in a situation where I might be asked an off-the-cuff question' (assumption)

'I must always make a good impression on my colleagues and superiors' (rule)

Coping strategies (trying to stay in control)

Overpreparing so his answers will please others

Nudging conversations in the desired direction

Leaving little time for questions at the end of team meetings

SPACE examples

1. **S**ocial context: asked by his boss for an overview on the progress of a current project

   Physiology: stomach tightening, heart pounding

   Action: keeps fidgeting in his chair

   Cognitions: 'I'm giving him too much detail, not the overview he wants. I'm rambling. He looks impatient. What's he thinking about me?'[1]

   Emotions: anxiety, embarrassment

2. **S**ocial context: asked a difficult question at the end of a team meeting, John speeds through an inadequate answer as he says he has to rush off to another meeting

   Physiology: stomach tightening, heart pounding

   Action: hurriedly collecting his papers and moving towards the door

   Cognitions: 'They know what I'm up to. I'm not fooling them. Why can't I just say "I'm not sure" or even "I don't know"?'[2]

   Emotions: anxiety, embarrassment

1 The coachee has the answer to his own question – 'I'm incompetent' (core belief).
2 To give these replies to his team would expose his incompetence.

Sometimes the coachee will provide a very economical case conceptualization that captures the thoughts, emotions and behaviours of their presenting problems, such as 'Trapped behind the mask'. They believed 'I always have to be on twenty-four-seven – bright, breezy and bubbly – as people expect it of me. It's exhausting'. Why they would be anxious about dropping their public persona and letting others see different aspects of their personality would be a subject for investigation. When coachees use metaphors, images and memorable phrases, it can be useful to revise them to include the goal, 'Allow people to see me, not the mask'.

John said after providing two SPACE examples that no more were needed as they would all be making the same point. In the SPACE examples, John put some of his situation-specific thoughts in the form of rhetorical questions such as 'What's he thinking about me?' In order to make explicit what's implicit in the question, the coach needs a clear and direct statement from the coachee:

Coach: What do you think he's thinking about you?
Coachee: Well, he probably doesn't have a high opinion of my presentation.
   [The answer isn't clear.]
Coach: What do you believe was his actual opinion of you in that situation?
Coachee: That I'm incompetent.

Flowing from the case conceptualization, goal-directed action plans are developed. Sarah's goal was to complete the 20-page report within the deadline and she accepted that several drafts would be needed, not the one draft with no mistakes she was fixated on. This acceptance of drafts stemmed from a comment the coach made in passing that 'no self-respecting writer would consider their first draft to be their best draft'. She took this comment to heart and the coach encouraged her to start making notes for the first draft in the session, which she did.

The goal for the second coachee, John, was to construct a view of himself as competent which he could believe in. The action plan would include looking for evidence of competence (past performance appraisals and promotions in the various companies he worked for) and developing performance standards that were realistic and reasonable with a focus on improvement, such as: learning to think on his feet rather than trying to avoid unanticipated questions; listening to conversations rather than trying to control their direction; and having a better balance between overview and detail when making presentations. He practised these three activities in the coaching sessions. Also, he revisited the comments of his first boss to determine if he (the boss) could capture the essence of John's capabilities and the course of his career in an ill-tempered outburst.

14

Structuring the coaching session

This means that each coaching session, following on from the assessment of the coachee's presenting issues, will follow a predictable pattern. This pattern is explained to the coachee as part of their continuing socialization (i.e. what's expected of them) into cognitive behavioural coaching (CBC). The structure of a CBC session is based on setting an agenda which is considered to be the best way of making optimum use of the time. The agenda items are jointly agreed through negotiation, but carrying out and reviewing extra-session tasks are permanent fixtures on the agenda. A typical agenda looks like this:

- Reviewing extra-session tasks: what learning did the coachee extract from carrying out the task? How did the coachee stop themself from undertaking the task? Whatever has occurred is of interest to the coach and therefore this review should not be divided into success or failure, but should be focused on learning. In fact, whatever happens in or out of the coaching session is grist to the CBC learning mill.
- Items for the current session: if the coachee has several concerns to discuss, then these should be prioritized rather than the session jumping from one to another. With each concern, the key thoughts, feelings and behaviours associated with it are identified. This jumping from topic to topic should also be avoided across sessions and a new topic for discussion is only selected when there is progress on the previous one. Coachees are encouraged to be succinct in discussing their issues so coaching does not get bogged down in long-winded storytelling detail

such as, 'He said, she said, they said, then I said . . .' Sometimes the coach can leapfrog coachee verbosity by asking, 'Can you put the key issue in a single sentence?' and, more often than not, the coachee can.

- Negotiating new extra-session tasks: what goal-related assignments does the coachee want to execute before the next session? If the coachee is unable to come up with suggestions, particularly in the early stages of coaching, the coach can suggest some. It's important that the coachee sees the connection between the task arising out of the session discussion and how it's related to their goal: session→task→goal.

- Summarizing the session: it's important that the coachee is encouraged to do this as the coach could misrepresent how the session went by saying, for example, 'We've made good progress today by identifying the beliefs that hold you back' while the coachee replies with an equivocal 'hmm' which the coach takes for agreement instead of seeking to clarify the reply (the coachee is not in agreement). Summaries occur throughout the session to check that coach and coachee are keeping in goal-directed step, and to provide feedback on improving the coaching alliance or detecting incipient difficulties within it.

- End-of-session feedback: what did the coachee find helpful and unhelpful about today's session? The second part of that question can prove anxiety- and anger-provoking for some coaches if they receive unflattering feedback such as, 'You were highly recommended but I'm afraid I'm very disappointed by what I've seen so far' or 'You seem to give an easy, slick reply to whatever I say to you. Are you really listening to me?' So these coaches would be trying to respond non-defensively to the coachee's comments while their minds are flooded with negative automatic thoughts (NATs) (e.g. 'I can't be any good as a coach' or 'How dare he say that when I'm trying so hard to help him?'). Their responses to these comments and other issues can be discussed in supervision (see Chapter 28).

If there are going to be any departures from the agenda, then both parties need to agree to it and a rationale advanced – how is the departure relevant to the current discussion about, for example, goals or tasks? This relevancy criterion acts as a check on the coach or coachee departing from the agenda any time something takes their interest and they want to pursue it.

15

Establishing goals

Once the coachee's concerns or problems have been clarified in the case conceptualization, the next step is to select goals – the desired outcomes the coachee wants to achieve. Selecting goals is not as easy as it may seem.

- The coachee may not understand the difference between control, 'I want to make my colleagues respect me' (that's up to them to decide) and influence, 'If I change certain aspects of my behaviour, then they might think more favourably of me' (this outcome could occur). Changing their behaviour is within their control; making others respect them is outside of their control.

- Choosing quick fix goals. The coachee says they want to learn to put up with their partner's often uncaring behaviour – 'You know, let sleeping dogs lie' – to avoid rows and uncomfortable silences. The real issue eventually emerged, namely, if they antagonized the partner by continuing to stand up for themself then the partner might 'abandon me'. The coachee changed their life coaching goal to drawing up a contingency plan for coping resourcefully with living alone if they were unable to make progress in their present relationship.

- Feeling calm or unmoved in the face of negative life events. This can be achieved if these events have absolutely no significance for the person. By definition, negative events trigger negative feelings because the coachee didn't want them to happen to them. By accepting their negative feelings, not trying to pretend they don't have them, they were able to express their disappointment about not getting the promotion and they would try again at a later date.

- Unrealistically high or low goals. The former would include goals outside of the person's current capabilities, such as 'I want to deliver a dazzling performance running my first workshop', when aiming for a competent one would be more appropriate and the workshop feedback can be used to improve it. The latter is aiming too low – 'I just want to pass. I'm not worried about grades' – in order to avoid feeling a failure if justified expectations of higher grades are not realized. Just passing brought relief but no sense of accomplishment. For a good performance, choose a difficult goal: 'This follows from the fact that people direct their behaviour towards goal achievement, so that difficult goals produce more effective behaviour than easy ones' (Arnold et al., 1995: 220–1).

- Putting the responsibility for goal achievement onto someone else, e.g. 'I can only stop smoking if my partner also quits', and thereby gives the coachee permission to continue smoking. They can stop independently of their partner if they commit themself to developing the self-control to deal not only with the psychological and physical discomfort they're likely to experience but also the temptations/provocations of being around someone who continues to smoke.

- Stating the goal in negative terms instead of positive ones, e.g. 'I want to stop being so defensive when I'm criticized.' So how does the person want to be when they're criticized? 'I want to assess criticism as objectively as I can: agreeing when it's accurate and disagreeing, with reasons, when it's not.' The next step is how to move from defensiveness to dispassion when assessing criticism. When coachees present negative goals, I usually say 'That's what you want to move away from, but turn round in your mind, so to speak, and tell me what it is you want to move towards'.

- Pragmatic or grit-your-teeth and get-on-with-it goals. The goal is neither interesting nor inspirational, but necessary to achieve. Here are some examples. The goal might be someone else's idea of what the person needs to achieve and they reluctantly go along with it but they do see the sense behind it (e.g. more exams in order to move up the career ladder). There is a clash between the person's 'should have' values (e.g. be slimmer and fitter) and actual values (e.g. 'I like eating whatever I fancy and detest exercise'), with the 'should have' values slowly, grudgingly gaining in importance due to the person's deteriorating health.

- Defining goals too early as 'very often the first things you talk about in a coaching session are not the real issues' (Greene and Grant, 2003: 127). For example, the coach may be too eager to focus on a feel-good goal – 'You can learn a few tips and techniques to manage that difficult team member more effectively. How does that sound?' – when the real issue emerges later: the coachee's avoidance of dealing with the team member 'as I feel overwhelmed in her presence as she has a very strong personality and she'll get the better of me in any exchange'.

- Goals for dealing with psychological blocks first, personal development goals later. Coachees often present exciting visions of how they want to be but don't deal with the psychological blocks that prevent these visions being translated into reality (I've worked with a few coachees who believed that if their vision was sufficiently powerful it would dissolve these blocks – only the hypothesis dissolved as it was unsupported by evidence).

Coachee: I want to feel much more comfortable and confident at meetings in presenting my ideas, listening to objections to them, engaging in vigorous debate, standing up for my ideas. All those kind of things.

Coach: What currently stops you from feeling comfortable and confident at meetings?

Coachee: Well, I worry about my ideas not being well received, shot down, dismissed as impracticable, that kind of thing. I'll be seen as foolish.

Coach: Are you actually presenting ideas at meetings?

Coachee: Only a few here and there. I'm reluctant to because of my worry.

Coach: So if you want to present more ideas, what do we need to deal with first?

Coachee: My worry about being seen as foolish.

- The goal regarding the coachee's psychological block was to present their ideas on a regular basis, accept that they can be welcomed, rejected, modified, improved – they're not fully formed at their conception – and to learn a new idea in coaching: that negative evaluation of some of their ideas at meetings does not have to lead to negative self-evaluation (see Chapter 20 for a model of dealing with psychological blocks).

- Stating the goal in general rather than specific terms, e.g. 'I want to be happier' rather than 'I want to sell my house and move to a new area in the next six months' and 'Be fitter so I can complete a half-marathon'. Achieving these goals are steps towards feeling happier. Specific goals are clear and measurable ones so the coachee can determine if they are making progress towards achieving them as well as enabling them to fine-tune their behaviour in order to increase their chances of goal success, e.g. regular training for the half-marathon, not just when they're in the mood.

Sometimes a coachee will want to talk in general terms – 'I want to think out loud about a situation I've got at work' – and doesn't want to be constrained by a goal-focused conversation. In this case, the cognitive behavioural coach with their clear-goals and clearly-defined-action-plans approach has to ask themself if they can adapt to this discursive conversation (if not, refer the coachee elsewhere). In longer-term developmental coaching, setting goals too early would inhibit the creation of a reflective space where the coachee is free to explore at length their often fundamental personal and professional concerns, for example, 'I'm no-nonsense, high energy, tough, results-oriented at work and I know I push myself too hard at times, but I'm a doormat at home. How can this be?' Through greater self-understanding, the coachee began to see the emergence of a new mindset that eventually led to the personal and professional changes they were seeking (when they became clearer about what they wanted, then they started setting themself clear and measurable goals).

Once goals have been agreed, they're not set in stone and can change in the light of incoming information (e.g. from the extra-session assignments), such as the coachee's goal is too ambitious and needs to be scaled back or they are making quicker progress than expected and want to capitalize on it by setting themself more challenging goals. Occasionally, a totally unexpected goal emerges. I was coaching someone to help him improve his performance in line with the company's goals when he suddenly announced, in our third session, that he hated his job, was going to resign and wanted to become a landscape gardener!

16

Teaching the cognitive model

During the first session of cognitive behavioural coaching (CBC), it's important for the coach to orient the coachee to their cognitive appraisals of events and associated emotional and behavioural reactions rather than engage in extended discussions about these events; in other words, to teach the cognitive model. Too much discussion about events can create the impression that events alone caused the coachee's reactions. The coach's judgement can determine the best time or moment to introduce the model. For example, the coachee might attend the first session late and say they're worried about their unpunctuality.

> *Coach:* What thoughts are going through your mind to lead to you being worried about getting to the first session late?
> *Coachee:* It creates a bad impression. You might think I'm undisciplined, disrespectful, not taking coaching seriously.
> *Coach:* What might you be thinking if you weren't worried about getting here late?
> *Coachee:* Something like I couldn't help the traffic jam. I'm paying for the session so if I turn up late, I have a shorter session. So what?
> *Coach:* Do you know what the point is I'm trying to make?
> *Coachee:* It's not so much getting here late but my thinking about getting here late.
> *Coach:* That's right, and we want to keep your thinking centre stage, so to speak, so we can relate it to the issues you want to discuss.

During the session the coachee might fall silent, become tearful, sigh deeply, react angrily to a question, or stare at the floor. Such moments can become opportunities for teaching the model by exploring the client's thinking with a 'What's going through your mind right now to make you sigh so deeply?' type question. These examples are meant to teach the model through the use of questions so that the coachee makes the thought–feeling connection themself rather than being told by the coach.

However, the coach can take a didactic stance in teaching the model (some coachees prefer direct explanations). You feel the way you think (Burns, 1999) might be the starting point.

Let me explain what I mean by that statement by giving you an example. Two people are vying for promotion. Both lose out. Now it's the same situation for both of them but one is angry because they believe they've been cheated out of what's rightfully theirs while the other person is disappointed because they tell themself it's unfortunate not to get it but there'll be other opportunities. It's not the situation itself that makes each person feel the way they do, but how each person *interprets* the situation that powerfully influences how they feel.

The coachee is then asked if they can relate this model to their own concerns such as feeling anxious about being landed with a three-year project:

> *Coachee:* Three years is a very long time to be kept in suspense as to whether the outcome will be success or failure.
> *Coach:* How do you see the outcome at the moment?
> *Coachee:* I see failure and that's why I'm so anxious. I know I shouldn't think that way, but I do. My boss wouldn't like to hear what I'm saying to you.

So, the person's mood keeps in step with their interpretations of the situation but, crucially, it's not the only interpretation that's available to them if they're prepared to widen their perspective to see what other ways there are of viewing and dealing with the situation (this 'widening of perspective' is the cognitive theme in coaching as it is in therapy). The thought–feeling link can be written on a whiteboard or flip chart in the coach's office in order to bring some order and clarity to the coachee's jumbled narrative:

Coach: We can distil from your story these three key CBC elements [writing on a flip chart]:

Situation	Thoughts	Emotions
One of your direct reports is rude to you	How dare he speak to me like that!	Angry
	He should respect me. I'm his boss.	
	He must have lost respect for me to talk to me like that.	Anxious
	Have I failed him in some way?	
	Do the rest of the team think like he does?	

Coachee: Sitting here and looking over there [pointing at the flip chart], I imagined all the thoughts were linked to anger, but I can now see the anxious thoughts are the more troubling because of their possible implications.

Coach: We might see these implications more clearly if you can translate your two rhetorical questions, which seem to imply an answer, into clear statements.

Coachee: Okay. The first one is 'I must have failed him in some way' and the second is 'If they think like he does, then I must be a lousy manager'. By the way, I don't believe I am a lousy manager just because he might be upset with me or that the rest of the team thinks in the same way that he does.

When individuals are able to step back from their upsetting thinking (called decentring in cognitive behavioural therapy [CBT]) and view it dispassionately – treating their thoughts and beliefs as opinions rather than as facts – some immediately start challenging their thoughts and beliefs without any prompting from the coach (as the coachee does with their last comment). However, the coach needs to be on the alert that some coachees might immediately disown their beliefs because they are embarrassed by or ashamed of them without any concurrent weakening in the conviction with which these beliefs are held.

It's important for the coach to remember that the coachee may say they understand the model but keep quiet about their disagreements (the mistake for the coach to make is to equate understanding with agreement), so any reservations, worries about or objections to the model need to be elicited. The coachee says the model can't be applied in some situations (these situations are 'mindless' – the coachee's mind plays no part in assigning meaning to them).

Coach: Could you give an example?

Coachee: Giving a presentation to the board is in and of itself an incredibly nerve-racking ordeal.

Coach: Could you be adding anything [tapping his forehead] to the presentation to turn it into an 'incredibly nerve-racking ordeal'?

Coachee: I don't think so. My colleagues all feel the same about making these presentations.

Coach: Have you carried out a survey to determine this?

Coachee: Not a survey! Colleagues make comments about it, that sort of thing.

Coach: Is there anything that makes it particularly nerve-racking for you?

Coachee: You're being judged. That's obvious, isn't it?

Coach: I presume they're judging your presentation, not you.

Coachee: You don't think that at the time.

[Personal meaning attached to the presentation is beginning to emerge.]

Coach: How do you think they're judging you as you're giving the presentation?

Coachee: Not good enough, falling short, they can see right through me.

Coach: Does this internal commentary distract you?

Coachee: I start stumbling over some words or pausing unnecessarily in the middle of sentences and I worry about that too.

Coach: Do you have any images flashing through you mind?

[The word 'cognitive' in CBC includes images which are just as important as thoughts and beliefs in conveying meaning.]

Coachee: Glimpses of losing my job, downsizing the house, taking the children out of private schools, losing friends, a gruesome downward spiral. It's hard to keep focused when you've got that lot going through your mind.

[An outpouring of meaning.]

Coach: Do you still believe that you make no contribution [tapping his forehead] to this 'incredibly nerve-racking ordeal'?

Coachee: Okay. I do make a contribution. I wonder why I was so determined not to see it.

The coachee believed, like some other coachees, that taking psychological responsibility for their unproductive reactions to events meant blaming themself ('I'm so stupid for behaving like that') which they wanted to avoid: responsibility→blame→ self-depreciation→distress. In CBC, psychological responsibility means taking ownership of one's thoughts, feelings and behaviours and making changes in those that interfere with goal-striving. Blame is not part of psychological responsibility: just an acknowledgement of the way things currently are and that different response options are now to be explored and the chosen ones implemented.

Other coachees may not be aware of what they're thinking in particular situations and can't be expected to take responsibility for thoughts they can't identify, but they may know how they feel. The coach asks the coachee to imagine vividly the situation:

Coachee: The team leader is asking everyone for their opinion and my turn is coming up. I'm feeling very anxious, agitated.

Coach: Explore that feeling in your mind's eye.

Coachee: Well, I'm sitting there desperately trying to think of something clever to say to impress the group. Nothing is coming, my mind is freezing. I'm getting more desperate as my turn gets ever closer.

Coach: What do you think will happen when it comes to your turn?

Coachee: I'll come across as a gibbering idiot, make a fool of myself.

Other ways to stimulate coachees' thinking include: asking what others might be thinking in similar situations to the coachee's; engaging in role play with the coach to try and recreate in the session the interpersonal difficulties the coachee is having, for example, with a colleague; asking what's the worst that could happen in a particular situation, and the coach suggesting the opposite of what they hypothesize are the coachee's actual thoughts (Beck, 2011):

> *Coachee:* When I'm talking to my boss, he sometimes takes off his glasses, puts them on the table, closes his eyes and rubs them. I feel uncomfortable when he does that.
> *Coach:* Do you know what you feel uncomfortable about?
> *Coachee:* I'm not sure.
> *Coach:* He might be doing that because you've given him some great ideas to consider.
> [Suggesting the opposite.]
> *Coachee:* I doubt it. When I look at him doing that I know what he's thinking, 'What's she doing wasting my time with this nonsense?'.
> [During the assessment, the coachee said she was vigilant for any signs that might indicate their work was being discredited.]

Taking psychological responsibility can be a very welcome development because it shows coachees that they don't have to rely on changing others or situations first before they can feel better or act differently which, if this was the case, would make personal change much more difficult to achieve. Therefore, it's important in CBC for psychological responsibility to be announced in the active voice, 'I make myself [e.g. anxious, angry] in that situation because I believe . . .' rather than continuing to use the passive voice, 'He/she/it makes me feel, think or act in that way'. Making statements in the active voice can leave some coachees feeling psychologically exposed:

> *Coachee:* It's like my protection has been removed: no more excuses, rationalizations. Blaming others can be comforting, pointing your finger at them instead of yourself. Feels kind of scary giving it up.

Coach: Any benefits in taking responsibility for how you respond to others, to events?

Coachee: I suppose the biggest benefit will be feeling that I'm more in control of my reactions and if I don't like a particular response I can learn to change it. I'm always blaming my boss for my moodiness when I get stressed and sometimes wish she was transferred somewhere else or even drop dead. Of course, her replacement could be worse than her.

Coach: Worse or better, you're still tying your mood, whether it goes up or down, to the kind of boss you have. Whatever kind of boss you have is outside of your control; moderating your moodiness is within your control.

Coachee: And that's what I want to learn in coaching.

[The coachee's moodiness was driven by their belief that their boss should always act reasonably towards them including not placing any undue pressure on them.]

The transition from passive to active voice is emphasized throughout coaching as part of the coachee's developing role as a self-coach with a concomitant sense of increased personal agency. That is, as self-limiting beliefs are dismantled and replaced with personal growth ones, this greater internal control enables the coachee to achieve more, gives them the confidence to tackle a wider range of troublesome situations (including the ones they've been avoiding), and they feel more optimistic about achieving goals they previously considered to be out of their reach.

17

Two key attributes of psychological health

Usually, books on coaching, leadership, sports psychology, positive psychology, and resilience provide lists of strengths, attributes or qualities that they deem to be essential for success in life (I do this in Chapter 26 on resilience). These lists can be extensive and each attribute is often described in a few sentences. Sometimes it can seem from, for example, the 10, 15 or 20 qualities described that you will never be able to develop all of them. Therefore, which ones are more important than others or are they all equally important? From the abundance of attributes on offer, I would like to select two which I believe are essential to psychological health and discuss them in depth: self-acceptance and high frustration tolerance (HFT).

17.1 *Self-acceptance*

Self-acceptance means accepting yourself, warts and all, and not attaching to yourself any global evaluations or ratings (positive or negative) as these cannot capture the complexity, changeability and uniqueness of the person you are. For instance, a person might label themself as a success when promoted and a failure when demoted. Do these words 'success' or 'failure' accurately and completely sum up the person as well as their life past, present and future? Some coachees will say 'I certainly feel like a failure' when they've experienced a setback such as not achieving an important goal (see emotional reasoning in Chapter 2). In this example, the person is making the part equals the whole error in reasoning: goal or behavioural failure = self-failure.

Self-acceptance means the person refuses to rate themself on the basis of their traits, actions, achievements and disappointments, but they do rate those aspects of themself that they wish to change. For instance, 'I can accept myself for acting impulsively at times which brings more problems than I would like. However, I'm working hard to remind myself to think before I act, so I wait 48 hours to see if it still seems like a good idea. It usually doesn't.' If the person condemns themself for being impulsive, then they give themself two problems for the price of one: impulsiveness (original problem) and self-depreciation ('I'm useless for acting impulsively' – added problem). 'How many problems do you want?' I ask my coachees. Sometimes, self-depreciation ('I'm incompetent for failing to secure a contract') leads to a chain of emotional and behavioural consequences such as feeling low, increased drinking, procrastination, irritability with colleagues, friends and family, lower productivity, poor sleep pattern, and some social withdrawal.

In the coaching session, I may open a pack of playing cards and place one card at a time on the table to graphically illustrate the sequence of problems flowing from self-depreciation. Some coachees buy a pack of cards and keep it unopened on their desk to remind themselves to remain focused on tackling their workload, not wasting time by opening the pack of cards, i.e. distracted by self-depreciation and its consequences. The bottom line is this: with self-acceptance – fewer problems; self-depreciation – more problems.

Self-acceptance doesn't mean complacency: if you can accept yourself, then why bother to struggle for anything in life? You can be as ambitious as you want, work as hard as you want, and with self-acceptance guiding the way you're unlikely to be overly worried about taking risks which might end in failure or rejection. Also, you're unlikely to let success go to your head as your personal worth is not tied to achieving it – successes and setbacks are not taken too seriously. If the person does act complacently about self-acceptance, it's unlikely they have understood the concept or absorbed it into their outlook.

To really understand and internalize it, they need to put themself into a range of situations – not ones where they might come to physical harm – where they're likely to be criticized, ridiculed or rejected; people are putting *them* down, not just criticizing their actions or attitudes. For example, giving their true opinions about various issues knowing that some members of their social group will verbally abuse them for holding these opinions, whereas previously they would have offered anodyne opinions to win approval and keep themself safe from verbal attack. Such actions, or lack of them, will enable the person to determine the strength of their conviction in self-acceptance: is it lip service or committed service they're demonstrating?

Internalizing self-acceptance provides long-term psychological stability, but not unwaveringly so, and quickens the process of self-righting (i.e. returning to normal functioning) when your life takes some unexpected knocks as you won't have to haul up your self-esteem from the low point to which it has fallen. You will know if you are deepening your conviction in self-acceptance as episodes of self-depreciation will become fewer over time (but don't expect elimination of them) and not last as long as previous ones did.

Talking of self-esteem, I'm not keen on helping people to raise self-esteem as what rises also falls when you make your self-worth conditional on certain requirements being present in your life, such as having lots of friends, a partner, respect of colleagues, achieving your ideal weight, well-behaved children, trying to look eternally young as you get older, or several holidays a year. If one or more of your desired conditions is absent from your life, you're likely to activate your negative core beliefs from their dormant state and become ensnared within them, for example, 'I've put on some weight. I'm repulsive'. Self-esteem is like an internal stock market: the value of your ego rising and falling depending on how your self-estimation is faring this week.

17.2 *High frustration tolerance*

The prospect of change is often more appealing than the hard work involved in achieving it. In order to ingrain new productive thoughts and behaviours, the person needs to develop high frustration toler-ance (HFT). This is the ability to endure in times of uncertainty, upheaval and distress without continually complaining how difficult the struggle is or lapsing into self-pity every time a new setback or difficulty is encountered. Considerable discomfort is to be expected and embraced *now*, without having to like it, in order to suffer less in the future as the person's problems start to be resolved through the effort they've applied to tackle them.

Ironically, people who avoid experiencing discomfort are demon-strating an unproductive form of HFT because they keep complaining about the discontents in their life but do little or nothing to deal with them – endurance without achieving any beneficial results.

The cognitive core of HFT is: 'I will tolerate discomfort and frustra-tion in order to reach my goals' – persistence with purpose. I don't ask my coachees if they feel comfortable about what they're going to do as this seems a counterproductive question: HFT doesn't develop by staying in your comfort zone, and a continual emphasis by the coach on 'Do you feel comfortable doing this?' type questions will not only ham-per coachees' progress but will also suggest that there is, after all, a way to change painlessly and easily which some coachees are hoping for.

Much more productive I find is to discuss with my coachees the benefits of acquiring HFT in order to increase the odds in their favour of achieving their goals. For example, coachees carry out extra-session tasks which involve giving themselves a daily dose of discomfort (DDD) – executing assignments which they perceive as boring, burdensome and unpleasant and have been avoiding for some time, such as getting on top of their paperwork or facing up to interpersonal conflict in order to try and resolve it. By immers-ing themselves in their discomfort and completing these DDD tasks, they discover how much more efficient their lives become:

People with high frustration tolerance are going to experience less stress, accomplish more, and feel better about themselves. Facing up to your frustrations, building tolerance for them, and acting to solve your problems associated with these feelings is a prime way to take charge of the way you'd prefer your life to go.
(Knaus, 2002: 46)

18

Action plans

When difficulties have been discussed (where the coachee is currently stuck) and reformulated as a goal (what the coachee would like to see happen), the next stage of coaching is to develop an action plan to reach that goal. If there are any psychological impediments to action planning/implementation, these will need to be dealt with first, such as a coachee believing that 'I must feel comfortable and in control before I start the action plan' (see Chapter 19). An action plan specifies the steps required to reach a goal. Each step needs to be clarified through a series of questions: What will I do? When will I do it? Where will I do it? How long do I propose to spend on it? What's the contingency plan if it proves too difficult to do? Other considerations for the coach to bear in mind are as follows.

- Assessing whether the coachee has the skills to execute the task, such as them wanting to act assertively in a specific context instead of their previous behaviour of either passivity or anger. As they don't understand what assertive behaviour is, in-session rehearsal of such behaviour would be required.
- Asking if the coachee is actually interested in the chosen task. The coach may overemphasize collecting data through form-filling, keeping diaries, and the coachee feels duty-bound to comply but collecting data through action assignments would be more stimulating for them.
- Helping the coachee to list several possible extra-session tasks, which may have emerged during the course of the session, rather than trying to identify just the one task near the end of

the session. Having a menu of tasks to choose from helps to increase the coachee's interest in and motivation to carry out the selected one.

- Negotiating challenging but not overwhelming tasks (Dryden and Neenan, 2015): assignments that are sufficiently stimulating to promote constructive change but not so daunting as to possibly inhibit coachees from carrying them out. The coachee may want to take on too much, too soon, driven by their perfectionist beliefs (e.g. 'I need to find an instant and comprehensive solution to my difficulties') or the coach may encourage the coachee to take early, overly ambitious steps so that rapid progress will demonstrate their talent as a coach (either way, the coachee is overwhelmed by the scale of the tasks). Alternatively, coaching proceeds too slowly as both parties want to minimize the experience of discomfort: the coachee carries out non-stretch tasks and the coach doesn't want to encourage them to push themself a little harder in case they get upset with them (either way, the coachee feels underwhelmed by their insubstantial progress).

In the following dialogue, the coach and coachee discuss what will be the latter's first step in their goal-directed action plan.

Coach: Can you remind me of your goal?
Coachee: To complete a series of boring tasks within the next three months. I've been avoiding them for a long time.
Coach: We've listed what these avoided tasks are and it's quite a list. And through this process of embracing discomfort you hope to . . .?
Coachee: Develop high frustration tolerance – grit my teeth and get stuck in! I want to make my life much more efficient.
Coach: So, what's your first step in your action plan for change?
Coachee: Well, I'm torn between spending the whole weekend clearing out the garage versus just starting small by vacuuming out my car.

Coach: Do you think you can jump from long-term avoidance to suddenly immersing yourself in a weekend of tedium?

Coachee: I very much doubt it. I suppose I'm just impatient to get on with it.

Coach: Do you see any benefits in being less ambitious at this stage?

Coachee: I suppose the obvious benefit is don't try to run before you can walk. I might find even vacuuming the car is too much boredom too soon.

Coach: What might be the danger in attempting to clear out the garage?

Coachee: Feeling overwhelmed by the immensity of the task I've set myself, giving up, feeling demoralized, seeing myself as a failure and maybe not coming back to coaching.

Coach: So, is the first step to vacuum the interior of your car? [coachee nods] When, where and what time will you do it?

Coachee: This Sunday afternoon at home at 2 p.m.

Coach: How much time will you spend on the task?

Coachee: I want to spend at least half an hour on it.

Coach: Any potential obstacles that might get in the way of you doing it?

Coachee: Just the usual one – I can't be bothered!

Coach: What will you do to be bothered and get on with it?

Coachee: I'm going to leave a big sign on the car over the week-end, 'I need to be vacuumed on Sunday at 2 p.m.'.

Coach: Good, and make a note of what happened on Sunday. We can get a lot of information from these early tasks: if they're too difficult, we can break them into smaller tasks; and if you complete them without much difficulty, you can set yourself bigger, harder tasks and thereby make quicker progress.

Coachee: Any tips for, hopefully, my first success?

Coach: I suggest to individuals who procrastinate like you've been doing to email me when they've done the task as it usually increases their motivation to do it.

Coachee: Okay. That will give me an extra incentive.

Coach: But I only suggest the email in the early stages of coaching as a motivational push. The key to success is you developing the internal motivation to complete all the tasks in your action plan without continual prodding from me.

Coachee: I understand.

[The coachee said they were so 'psyched up' on Sunday that they started the task at 7.30 a.m. and had the car cleaned, not just vacuumed, by 9 a.m. Thereafter, they moved fairly rapidly through their list of avoided tasks and had them all completed within the three-month period they'd set themself.]

Leahy (2005) says there are three steps to personal empowerment:

1. What is my goal?
2. What do I have to do to get it?
3. Am I willing to do it?

The goal-related extra-session tasks – the work between the coaching sessions – will test that willingness. Carrying out these tasks is essential to the success of cognitive behavioural coaching (CBC). The evidence from the cognitive behavioural therapy (CBT) research literature (e.g. Kazantzis et al., 2005) shows that those clients who carry out these tasks make greater gains than those who don't, which might seem common sense to many readers (CBT likes to have empirical support for its claims).

The coaching session is a poor arena for assessing change because of its removal from the client's everyday experience. These tasks allow clients to test and change unhelpful thoughts and behaviours in the real-life situations where their difficulties occur, deepen their conviction in their new problem-solving outlook, and learn and apply new skills with increasing competence and confidence.

Sufficient time should be left at the end of the session to discuss these tasks and they should be written down in clear, concrete terms and the coach and coachee should both have a copy of them (see Table 18.1; the first three columns are filled out in the session).

Written tasks reduce considerably any misunderstandings which might occur if these tasks are communicated only verbally. It's important for the coachee to see how the task arises from discussion in the session and is linked to their goal: session→task→goal. Lastly, whether these tasks are carried out fully, partially or not at all, the focus is on continual learning, not success or failure. Tompkins (2004) suggests five Cs for reviewing extra-session tasks.

1. Be consistent – review these tasks in every session (this is done at the beginning of the session).
2. Be curious – adopt an open-minded, non-judgemental approach to reviewing the tasks, particularly if the coachee has not completed them.
3. Be complimentary – no matter how small the effort was in attempting to carry out the task.
4. Be careful – don't reinforce task non-completion by pretending it doesn't matter.
5. Consider changing or repeating the task depending on the information that has emerged from this examination.

Coaches need to monitor their own reactions if coachees don't carry out the agreed tasks, such as feeling angry because 'he's not taking coaching seriously' or feeling anxious because continuing non-compliance with task execution means 'I'm failing as a coach because a really good coach would have sorted it out by now'. The coach, with the aid of a competent supervisor, needs to step back from their thoughts and feelings and find more productive responses (see Chapter 28). In a spirit of open-mindedness, the coach asks their coachee what the problem might be, and the response is: 'Now you ask, every time I suggest the task you always find fault with it and, as always, your suggestion is the better one. So I'm not eager to carry out your task. That's why.' The coach apologizes and the coachee's suggestions now lead the way unless the coach, but not in a ceaselessly fault-finding way, sees potential difficulties with a few of the coachee's suggestions.

Table 18.1 Extra-session task form

What is the task? (State when, where, how often and how long the task is to be carried out)	What is the purpose of the task? (This should follow on from the work done in the session and be linked to the coachee's goal)	Troubleshooting obstacles to task completion	Did you complete the agreed task? If not, how did you prevent yourself from carrying it out?
		Potential obstacle: Response:	

19

Beliefs which interfere with carrying out extra-session tasks

The coachee's commitment to change and the hard work associated with it may be undermined by six major self-defeating and goal-blocking beliefs (Neenan and Dryden, 2014).

1. *'I cannot take constructive action until I can be certain of success'*
    Wanting to know how the journey ends before taking the first step means there's no point in putting on your walking shoes. People who worry about uncertainty 'equate the unknown with danger. However, uncertainty is actually *neutral* with regard to outcome' (Leahy, 2005: 105; emphasis in original). In other words, there could be a range of outcomes to consider instead of the person being fixated on only one: failure. Doubt and uncertainty are the usual concomitants of change and therefore require acceptance of their presence rather than fear of what you think they portend.

2. *'I cannot take constructive action until I feel comfortable to do so'*
    If you believe that only when you feel comfortable will you be able to start the change process, then the starting date will recede into the distant future. If you're not looking forward to carrying out a particular task, then why should you feel comfortable about doing it? When you start to take constructive action, you will feel uncomfortable as you're now facing your difficulties rather than avoiding them. Yet as Ellis (2002: 155) states: 'Make yourself do the work you dislike, force yourself to do it and do it. Deliberately push yourself to be uncomfortable – yes,

uncomfortable – until you finally find the work easy and comfortable.' In a nutshell, discomfort first, comfort later.

3. *'I cannot take constructive action because I don't have a sense of control'*

Coachees who believe they must be in full control of their responses to events are actually reinforcing their fear of losing control as well as how they will be judged by others, 'My colleagues will think I'm weak'. Demanding self-control is the illusion of control. Real control means not being afraid of losing it, being self-accepting, not self-condemning, when this loss occurs, and looking for constructive ways to regain it. For example, a coachee who dreaded being the centre of attention because they would start blushing 'and show myself up as nervous and pathetic' eventually decided to accept, rather than try to suppress, their blushing: 'If I blush, so be it.' They started putting themself in situations where they would be the centre of attention, e.g. speaking up at meetings, asking questions at workshops. Their blushing was evident to others but the coachee discovered, to their delight, that the frequency, intensity and duration of their blushing episodes decreased dramatically once they'd internalized this 'control through acceptance' strategy.

4. *'I cannot act differently because I don't feel competent yet'*

Competence is not usually achieved in one fell swoop. Trial and error is the normal procedure, so expect to act incompetently. Through conscious awareness of what you're doing wrong, correcting your mistakes and persistent practice of the new behaviour or skills, you will eventually learn to act competently. That's how it's done. It's highly unlikely that you will be able to avoid this learning process ('How do I become instantly competent?') and the time wasted in trying to find an answer to this unrealistic question could have been spent productively learning how to move from incompetent to competent behaviour.

5. *'I cannot take new action which is strange to me because I don't feel confident to do so'*

It's perfectly natural to feel unconfident when acting in new and strange ways; sometimes a coachee will proclaim 'But this isn't me!' This dissonant state – the conflict or disharmony between old and new ways of thinking, feeling and acting – can lead to some coachees leaving coaching in order to feel natural again, but they return to the status quo in their lives which they were keen to change a few weeks or months earlier. Accepting and persisting with this dissonant state until it passes means that new habits become ingrained and old habits now seem unfamiliar. Hauck (1982) likens this dissonant state to wearing in a new pair of shoes.

6. '*I cannot undertake constructive actions, particularly those which are risky for me, because I don't have the courage to do so*'
   Going after what you want in life involves some risk, including the prospect of failure and rejection. Courage means doing things that you're afraid of without giving way to the fear, such as setting up your own business, public speaking or asking someone for a date. Building courage in facing your fears comes from taking action, not waiting for courage to arrive miraculously and then you can get started. Familiar expressions such as 'pluck up courage' and 'take one's courage in both hands' exhort doing, not delaying. The longer you wait for courage to arrive, the more likely you are to convince yourself 'I haven't got the guts to take these chances' and settle for second-best in life.

With all six beliefs, there's a common theme linking them: desirable conditions have to exist *before* constructive action can be undertaken. This is putting-the-cart-before-the-horse thinking. If you want to feel certain, comfortable, in control, act competently, confidently and courageously, then you first need to feel uncertain, uncomfortable, not in control, and to act incompetently, unconfidently and uncourageously. Accepting this paradox of personal change is one less obstacle on the road to goal achievement.

20

Dealing with psychological blocks to change

I mentioned in the Introduction that cognitive behavioural coaching (CBC) has two main elements: goal achievement and dealing with psychological blocks if they emerge. When these blocks interfere with goal-striving, coachees can be shown the ABCDE model of psychological problem solving (Ellis and MacLaren, 1998):

A = activating event or adversity

B = beliefs about A

C = emotional and behavioural consequences of holding these beliefs

D = distancing oneself from these beliefs in order to gain objectivity before discussing them (the model stipulates disputing beliefs which can unfortunately inject an adversarial tension into coaching or therapy relationships, so I prefer the term 'discussion')

E = effective new outlook

For example, a therapist said they were anxious (C) when thinking about adding coaching to their private practice (A) because 'I must be certain I will be successful as a coach' (B). The coachee's beliefs were discussed (D) along the lines shown in the sections below (these are not the only discussion points). The questions are closed to focus the coachee's mind on whether their beliefs assist goal-striving; then discussion flows from their replies (see Table 20.1).

20.1 *Is your belief rigid or flexible?*

This is the difference between a fixed outlook (a prisoner of your beliefs) and one based on personal and professional growth: rigid thinking restricts such growth; flexible thinking promotes it. The therapist was demanding to know the unknowable before venturing into coaching rather than accepting the risks and being open-minded about the outcome.

20.2 *Is your belief realistic or unrealistic?*

Does the person's subjective view of the situation correspond with the facts of the situation? Reality doesn't reshape itself to meet the therapist's demand to know the outcome before it has occurred, so their belief is inconsistent with reality. The further the person's viewpoint diverges from empirical reality the more likely they are to perpetuate their psychological difficulties.

20.3 *Is your belief helpful or unhelpful?*

This looks at the practical consequences of holding on to a belief. Are there more costs or benefits from the belief? The therapist said the major benefit in demanding certainty of outcome shielded them from possible, and when really worried, probable failure. The major cost was that furthering their career was now blocked by this belief, which led to frustration and anger with themself for being so timid, particularly when other therapists they knew were developing successful coaching practices without making similar demands. They eventually reformulated the major benefit as another major cost in stifling their desire to become a coach.

20.4 *Would you teach your belief to others?*

If a person thinks their belief is reasonable – it makes good sense to them – would they teach it to their family, friends and colleagues? The answer is almost always 'No'. The therapist said they wouldn't teach it to others because it would hold you back in life and make you fearful about doing anything important or adventurous because you can't be certain of the outcome. If they wouldn't teach it to others, then why do they continue to teach it to themself? If a coachee did say 'Yes', then what might the implications be for these others in internalizing this belief?

Through discussions such as these, the coachee constructed a flexible, goal-oriented belief (E): 'I will take the risk even if it ends in failure rather than not take the risk and deeply regret it, so I will focus my energies on doing my best to establish a coaching practice.' Examining a coachee's self-limiting beliefs and developing self-helping alternatives has benefits in terms of neuroplasticity: the lifelong ability of our brains to reorganize neural pathways in the light of our actions and experiences: 'The mere act of considering an alternative interpretation of a well-worn automatic negative thought [e.g. 'I know I'll get it wrong because I'm stupid'] can, over time, help reduce the power of that thought by reducing the strength of its representation in cognitive neural networks' (Treadway, 2015: 95).

The first step in the therapist's action plan was to sign up for a coaching course to gain some qualifications. Also, every day for 15 minutes they flooded their mind with anxiety, 'I'm not sure I'm going to be successful'. After a week of doing this flooding technique (Leahy, 2017), they became bored with worrying about uncertainty and their anxiety declined to minimal.

Table 20.1 The ABCDE model of psychological problem solving

A = activating event	B = beliefs	C = consequences	D = discussion (outcome)	E = effective new outlook
Thinking about adding coaching to my private practice but seeing possible failure ahead.	I must be certain I will be successful as a coach before I make a decision.	Anxiety. Procrastination about making a decision to extend their practice.	My belief is rigid as it gives me no options to pursue. My colleagues are moving on and I'm staying stuck. It's unrealistic. This is not how the world works. I'd never get out of bed in the morning if I had to know in advance how the day ends. My belief is definitely not going to help me achieve my goal and I certainly wouldn't teach this nonsense to others.	I will take the risk even if it ends in failure rather than not take the risk and deeply regret it. So I will focus my energies on doing my best to establish a coaching practice.

21

Practical problem-solving model

The early focus in cognitive behavioural coaching (CBC) is on developing goal-related action plans unless psychological blocks intrude (see Chapter 20). There are a number of practical problem-solving models available and the one I use here is ADAPT (Nezu et al., 2007).

Rosemary had a business client who often got angry and shouted at her during contract negotiations. She tried to placate him during these outbursts and didn't challenge any of his accusations because, if she did, she feared she could lose his business and his company was one of her biggest clients. She wondered at times if she was somehow responsible for his behaviour, if he was naturally even-tempered until he met her and was 'forced' by her manner into being bad-tempered. However, shortly before she came for coaching, she decided 'enough was enough' and she was now prepared to stand up for herself even if it meant losing his business: 'I'm not going to allow myself to be spoken to in that way any longer.'

A = attitude: I'm now mentally prepared to deal with this issue. I feel optimistic about finding a solution.

D = defining the problem and setting a realistic goal: The problem has been allowing him to shout at me because I didn't object to it. He does it a lot – he has a short fuse – so it's likely to be difficult to get him to stop. My goal is for the meetings to be conducted in a professional manner, with give and take on both sides, but no shouting.

A = generating alternative solutions: So in what ways can I attempt to achieve my goal? Well I could [making a list]:

1. Tell him that losing his temper is no longer acceptable and that time-outs will be called when he starts getting angry.
2. Try to find out why he loses his temper.
3. Explain to him why I've been so passive in the meetings and hope he will understand and agree with my new approach.
4. Phone or email him to let him know the conditions for the next meeting.
5. Suspend contract negotiations until he gets control of his temper.

P = predicting the consequences and developing a solution plan: What are the likely consequences for each alternative solution in helping me to reach my goal, and will I be able to carry out the chosen solutions? First, let me evaluate the possible solutions [a usefulness scale of 0–10 can be used for each solution where 0 is the least useful and 10 the most useful]:

1. This could be a good idea. Hopefully, he'll feel embarrassed when I suggest the time-outs as if he's a misbehaving child who needs time on his own to get control of himself. 7
2. Yes. This might bring something to light that we need to discuss, but I'm definitely not his therapist. 7
3. I'm not going to seek his approval as I will put myself back into a subordinate position. No way! 0
4. Yes. I will contact him to inform him of the new conditions within which the meeting will be conducted and in this way let him know that the worm has indeed turned. 8
5. I will move to this option if the time-outs don't work. 6

I'll try points 1, 2 and 4 and combine them in one solution. Yes, I do believe I will be able to carry it out and I don't see any blocks preventing me from doing it. In fact, I'm looking forward to my next meeting with him.

T = trying out the solution to see if it works: Well, I did phone him and told him what would happen if he lost his temper.

He got a bit grumpy and said I didn't make my points clear at the meetings, so I said I would do my best to rectify this if he told me non-angrily which points they were. At the meetings when he started to get grumpy and blunt in his comments, I suggested a short break so he could regain his self-control and act in a more professional manner. He didn't want a break and his grumpiness and bluntness quickly disappeared. I think he was embarrassed that I was staying in control, not being placatory any more, and he seemed out of control. Anyway, he never apologized for his angry outbursts but eventually I got the contract. I wouldn't have been upset if I'd lost it because I've made some welcome changes in myself. You know, in the end I won three contracts: rewrote my own contract to stop blaming myself for his behaviour; successfully renegotiated the contract regarding his behaviour at the meetings; and then won the business contract. Not bad at all.

If the initial solutions that are tried are unsuccessful, the coachee can experiment with other ones on their list or think of new ones, including those provided by friends and colleagues. It's important that any potential solution is given a sufficient trial (not just one attempt) before declaring it unsuccessful. For example, if the time-outs offered by Rosemary hadn't worked the first time in calming him down, she said she would have used them a few more times before considering suspending contract negotiations, a more serious step to take.

Also, if some coachees are becoming psychologically agitated at the slow progress they're making, they might need to go back to the ABCDE model demonstrated in Chapter 20 to pinpoint and deal with their distress-producing beliefs; for example, 'Nothing works. I shouldn't have to struggle this damn hard to find a solution! Problem solving always seems so easy and straightforward in the bloody textbooks'. If 'nothing works' is true, then the coachee cannot be helped; something usually works if the coachee is open-minded and committed to finding out what it is.

22

Socratic questioning

Socratic questioning has been called a cornerstone of cognitive behavioural therapy (CBT; Padesky and Greenberger, 1995). It is derived from the Greek philosopher Socrates, who sought to reveal 'the truth by means of questions aimed at opening out what is already implicitly known, or at exposing the contradictions and muddles of an opponent's position' (Blackburn, 2016: 133). In CBT, Socratic questioning is a method of guided discovery whereby the therapist's questions encourage clients to step back from their problematic thinking in order to examine it objectively in terms of accuracy and usefulness (another method of guided discovery is behavioural experiments, see Chapter 23). This examination helps clients to develop more helpful attitudes and actions to aid problem solving and goal achievement. Through Socratic questioning, people are able to reach their own conclusions rather than being told what these should be by the questioner. Telling coachees the answers can be counterproductive:

- They might find them unhelpful and some coachees will be unwilling to say so.
- They may see them as standard answers rather than tailored to their particular concerns.
- They may believe ideas are being imposed upon them as the coach seeks to establish their authority and/or parade their 'wisdom'; also, the coach is signalling that they have nothing to learn from the coachee.
- It undermines the spirit and practice of collaborative empiricism, i.e. co-investigators in problem solving (see Chapter 10). Ledley et al. (2010: 86) suggest that 'the stance of collaborative

empiricism is perhaps best exhibited when the clinician uses the technique of Socratic questioning' rather than them attempting to make authoritative-sounding interpretations of the person's thoughts, feelings and behaviours.

- It encourages mental laziness as the coachee waits for the next problem-solving titbit to be served up by the coach.
- It weakens the coachee's ability to develop as a self-coach, i.e. function as an independent problem solver.

Individuals usually feel a greater sense of ownership of their new ideas if they're encouraged 'to let their brains take the strain' and think things through for themselves, aided by the coach's prompts (Dryden and Neenan, 2015). In the following dialogue, the coach resists the urge to provide answers:

Coachee: I'm not sure what to do with this issue. What do you suggest?

Coach: Just remind me of the issue.

Coachee: This team member provides first-rate information when I and others ask for help, but her manner is so superior and dismissive, as if I'm her intellectual inferior, can't work it out for myself and am interrupting her valuable work. She's highly respected, but not liked.

Coach: What's the problem for you if she 'provides first-rate information' when you ask for help?

Coachee: Well it's the manner in which she provides it. Makes you feel as if you're stupid.

Coach: Do you believe you're stupid for asking for her help?

Coachee: I don't think so. Mind you, she rarely asks for help from other team members.

Coach: Are you making a comparison between you asking for help more frequently and she rarely?

Coachee: Hmm. [ponders] I suppose I do see myself as a little stupid for asking her. I hadn't considered that before.

Coach: So is the idea in your mind before you speak to her rather than her making you feel stupid?

Coachee: It's in my mind already. I wish it wasn't.

Coach: Have you got any idea why you see yourself as a 'little stupid for asking her'?

Coachee: Not at the moment, as it's a surprise to me. I'll need to have a good think about it before our next session. But I still don't like her manner! Not that she'd pay any attention if I said that to her.

Coach: What's the more important element in your interaction with her?

Coachee: Well, obviously the first-rate information she provides, as I said.

Coach: Why is that not enough for you?

Coachee: Well, she could be pleasant too, couldn't she?

Coach: Do you want to stop asking for help until she develops a pleasant manner?

Coachee: No, that would be ridiculous. I suppose I want the information with jam on it. The information is the most important thing. I'll just put up with her manner. By the way, I notice you didn't make any suggestions when I asked you to. Why was that?

Coach: Through my questions, I was hoping to stimulate your thinking on the matter.

Coachee: Well, it certainly did. I'm intrigued why I'm linking asking for help to stupidity.

Coach: And you're going to bring some ideas about it to the next session. Right? [client nods]

Questions other than Socratic ones are also useful, such as:

- Closed ones to focus the coachee's reply, e.g. 'Is your belief rigid or flexible?' which was asked in Chapter 20 to initiate discussion, and then Socratic questions can be used to explore the answer, such as: 'How is your belief flexible, not rigid, if it doesn't provide you with any other options if your plans don't work out?'
- Confirm what the other person has said, e.g. 'So, if I've heard this right, the sticking point for you is your manager's refusal to apologize to you'.

- Clarifying coachee statements, e.g. 'What exactly did he do that triggered your angry outburst?'
- Direct questions to gather assessment information, e.g. 'How many times have you been late for meetings in the last two months?'
- Leading questions to test the coach's assumptions, e.g. 'It sounds as if you're worried about being seen as weak if you admit your nervousness to others. Is that accurate?'

Stanier (2016) says the best coaching question in the world is the AWE question: 'And what else?' This provides more options, rather than either/or alternatives, and can lead to better coachee decisions; it encourages the coach to exercise self-restraint by not automatically jumping in to give advice; and if the coach is uncertain where to go next in the conversation, asking the AWE question gives them more time to think. Obviously, the coach doesn't want to keep parroting 'And what else?' so, 'if you can feel the energy going out of the conversation, you know it's time to move on from this angle. A strong "wrap it up" variation of "And what else?" is "Is there anything else?"' (Stanier, 2016: 63).

In supervising the work of coaches over the years, I've noticed how many of them are uncomfortable with the coachee's silence following their questions as if silence denotes, for example, the coach's incompetence, progress isn't being made or the coachee is being subjected to unnecessary mental struggle. To cope with their discomfort, coaches might quickly end the silence with verbal 'noise' such as 'How are you doing with the question?' or offer their own answer to the coachee.

Trying to expunge silence from the session is a fundamental error because to 'start talking to fill the pause and to rescue the client from the discomfort of this awkward . . . situation . . . would be a mistake . . . as it interrupts the client's thought processes and disrupts the purpose of the Socratic question' (DiGiuseppe, 1991: 184). The coach might also attempt to end the silence by asking further questions, thereby hoping to 'nudge' the coachee into giving an answer: 'Could it be that your real worry is lack of support at the meeting for your ideas or is it that Bill is going to try and tear down your ideas as he's very confrontational?' Again, this tactic disrupts the Socratic process as each new question undermines the purpose of asking the previous one and the coachee's thinking time is 'crowded out' with several questions competing for their attention.

Also, the coachee might be experiencing cognitive dissonance (i.e. psychological tension arises when a person's beliefs contradict each other or their behaviour) triggered by the coach's question: 'You say you'll do whatever it takes to deal with this issue yet you don't carry out the agreed goal-related tasks. So what stops intent and action keeping in step?' The coachee's struggle to answer this question might reveal their blocks to change, for instance, 'My head wants the change but my heart is doubtful', and their doubts can be explored. Bringing their psychological struggle to a premature conclusion might have resulted in 'I don't know'.

Sometimes sufficient thinking time has been given but the coachee's replies are a mixture of: 'I don't knows'; 'It depends . . .', without specifying at least what some of the controlling or determining factors are; lacklustre responses such as 'Yeah, I suppose so'; or seemingly positive but actually empty statements of intent, 'You've just got to get on with it, haven't you?' In these circumstances, the coach can ask the coachee to verbalize how they processed the question (the coach's hypothesis is that the coachee didn't spend much time thinking about their question through lack of mental effort):

Coachee: The answer wasn't there. What else can I say?
Coach: Do you mean the answer didn't pop into your mind immediately or after several minutes of searching for one?
Coachee: Well, it didn't come straightaway, so I gave up.
Coach: Do you know why you give up so quickly?
Coachee: I don't know.
Coach: Have you just given up quickly again?
Coachee: I guess I have.

Coach: How about if we spend the rest of the session asking each other questions and saying out loud how we're processing the questions and what might block the way to finding an answer without either of us saying 'I don't know'?

Coachee: Okay. I'll give it a try.

Of course, the coachee's unproductive replies could be the result of the coach's long-winded, complicated, unclear questions, asking too many interrogatory 'Why?' questions, or the coachee doesn't have the knowledge to answer the question. For example:

Coach: What are your core values?

Coachee: I don't know. I'm not sure I know what a core value is.

[The coach could have asked: 'Do you know what core values are?']

However, having said all of the above, the coach shouldn't get stuck in Socratic mode if it becomes clear that some coachees require clear and direct explanations of how to solve their problems because they find Socratic questioning tiring, irritating and unproductive: 'Why should I rack my brains searching for answers to this problem when I know you've got some good ideas. Suggest some, then I'll comment upon them.' If the coachee likes one of the suggestions, then they should be asked if they're going to take ownership of it – 'Yes I am'. This is an important step to take in case they say at the next session, 'Your suggestion didn't work!' Remind them of their ownership of the suggestion and ask pointedly, 'How did *you* not make *your* suggestion work?' (adapted from Hauck, 1980).

23

Behavioural experiments

Behavioural experiments serve a cognitive purpose: to test the validity of the client's thoughts and beliefs through action assignments. The information gathered from experiments helps clients to develop new helpful beliefs and weaken/undermine existing unhelpful ones. Using reason to explore and expose the self-defeating nature of the person's troublesome thoughts is often intellectually persuasive in making the case for change, but they remain convinced at a deeper, emotional level that these thoughts are actually true. Testing these thoughts in the situations where the person's difficulties occur and developing new ideas and behaviours to address them, allows their head and heart to keep in step in believing in the effectiveness of these new responses.

For example, a coachee who described himself as a 'perfectionist' said that he dreaded making mistakes in those areas of his life where he believed his credibility was at stake, such as running workshops for companies – 'If I don't perform perfectly, then people will see me as useless, think that I don't know my subject and business will dry up'. Logically, this means that if the premise is true, not performing perfectly, then the conclusion must be true, no more business (coachees' premises frequently reveal errors of reasoning and therefore their conclusions can't be considered to be true). However, the coachee's continual striving to reach these perfectionist standards was 'wearing me out' and he was ready to 'break the tyranny of my standards'. He understood and accepted the rationale for behavioural experiments. What would he be prepared to do?

Coachee: My big fear is saying 'I don't know' to a question. I could say that deliberately and see what happens.
Coach: If that's your big fear, is that moving too fast, too soon?

Coachee: No, I want to try it.

Coach: Okay. We need to formulate the fear in a way that can be tested, such as 'If I say "I don't know" to a question from the audience, then . . . what?'

Coachee: Then it will be terrible.

Coach: We need to be specific about what 'terrible' refers to.

Coachee: The scores on the evaluations forms, or most of them, will be in the twos and threes – which they never have been – and the company won't ask me back to do any more workshops.

Coach: So the idea to be tested is 'If I say "I don't know" to a question, then most of the scores on my evaluation forms will be in the twos and threes and the company won't ask me to do any more workshops'.

Coachee: That's correct. [ponders] Logically, I know [tapping his head] that not being able to answer a question won't make me inadequate or bring about these consequences I fear, but it's not so easy to convince myself down here [pointing to his stomach] as it's already in knots just talking about it. Is the experiment designed to show that my fears are unfounded?

Coach: If you know the answer before an experiment is carried out, then it's not an experiment.

Coachee: [laughs] Of course!

Coach: One last thing: what might you do if you don't carry out the experiment?

Coachee: See myself as a failure?

Coach: That wouldn't be helpful or accurate. Experiments are carried out in an open-minded way to gather further information for discussion; they're not conducted in order to judge individuals on how well or badly they carried them out.

Coachee: Point taken. If I don't do it, I'll make some notes as to what stopped me which we can discuss at the next session.

Coach: That's fine.

When carrying out experiments, it's vitally important for the coachee to remember that he needs to be interested in learning from *whatever* the outcome is, not fixated on success or failure. If the experiment has to turn out in a predetermined way, then it's not an experiment as pointed out in the above dialogue. Information gleaned from experiments can, for example, reveal new aspects of the problem which then help to refine the case conceptualization (see Chapter 13) or the coachee wants to capitalize on his 'it went well' outcome to speed his progress through the action plan.

When the coachee said 'I don't know' at the workshop, there were no shock waves from the audience and the heavens didn't fall. The evaluations hardly varied from previous ones and he was offered further workshops to present. Just to prove to himself that the success of the experiment wasn't a fluke, he carried out further ones where he exposed his 'flaws'. These included:

- 'If they [the audience] see my hand shaking while I drink a glass of water, then they'll think I'm nervous and therefore weak and despise me.'
- 'If I use a word or two incorrectly, then they'll think I'm stupid and not be able to trust what I'm saying.'
- 'If I have to try several marker pens before finding a useable one, then they'll see me as ill-prepared, not on top of things.'
- 'If I say I sometimes get nervous presenting workshops, then I'll be reported as an unfit presenter who's shaking in his shoes.'

None of the coachee's fears were realized on the evaluation forms; the scores remained high and the workshops kept coming. What had he learnt from these experiments?

Coachee: It's impossible to remove all weaknesses from my character or mistakes from my performance. Of course, I made mistakes before in workshops but I prayed they wouldn't be noticed, which just maintained my fears. With these experiments, I was deliberately exposing my imperfections to see if they would lead to rejection in terms of further work. I greatly overestimated how critical and unforgiving people would be of my mistakes. Obviously, I was the most critical and unforgiving person of my mistakes. I'm more relaxed now than I've ever been in running workshops and if I trip over my feet or say 'I don't know', too bad. I'm an expert in my field, but in the dictionary definition sense of being very knowledgeable, no longer in the perfectionist sense of endlessly striving to be completely knowledgeable so I won't be caught out and exposed as useless.

Behavioural experiments don't have to start with testing the validity of the coachee's old assumptions. Mooney and Padesky (2000) suggest a number of advantages if the focus is on constructing new assumptions:

1. Changes occur more quickly.
2. The collaborative process is creative rather than revisionist, i.e. creating new possibilities, not modifying old thinking traps.
3. The person's motivation and interest are increased.
4. More change may occur if there is a wider range of possibilities on offer instead of the constricted vision offered by focusing on old patterns of behaviour.

However, the coach should discuss with their coachee the different ways behavioural experiments can be used rather than assume they want to be creative rather than revisionist. For example, the coachee in the above dialogue could have tested straightaway a new assumption about saying 'I don't know': 'If I say "I don't know" then this could be the first welcome step in loosening the grip of my perfectionist thinking and I very much doubt this admission will adversely affect my evaluation scores or offers of further work from the company'. The coachee wanted to test his old fear-laden assumptions rather than new, more hopeful ones, but through his chosen route he eventually developed a balanced and realistic assessment of his abilities.

Another way to carry out behavioural experiments is to test both the old and new versions of the 'I don't know' belief at the same time to determine which version's predictions are more accurate. The coachee also carried out other kinds of experiments based on observation (attending colleagues' workshops to see how they handled difficult questions and coped with any setbacks) and conducting a survey among his colleagues to see if they were driven by similar perfectionist standards.

> *Coachee:* The feedback from my colleagues was that you can't know your subject 100 per cent and that you don't need to strive to be perfect to have a successful career or get work from companies. I'm coming round to their point of view.

Also, if coachees have no clear 'if... then' assumptions to test, they can carry out discovery behavioural experiments (Kennerley et al., 2017) where the guiding principle is 'Let's see what happens if I do this', for instance, the coachee is the first to give their opinion at a meeting when they usually wait for others to go first. Experiments can also be conducted in the session if the opportunity arises:

> *Coach:* You say you keep putting off contacting a friend you haven't seen for several years.
> *Coachee:* Yes. I'm anxious in case she doesn't want to see me and I'll feel a fool contacting her again.
> *Coach:* Could there be another outcome?
> *Coachee:* Well, she might want to see me.
> *Coach:* How do we find out which prediction is more accurate?
> *Coachee:* Obviously contact her.
> *Coach:* Do you want to phone her right now?
> *Coachee:* Okay. I'm nervous ... deep breath ... go for it. [gets mobile phone out of her bag]

The coachee's friend agreed to meet for coffee and their relationship resumed.

Coaches can use a form to guide their coachees through behavioural experiments (see Table 23.1). Butler et al. (2008: 109) state that behavioural experiments engage the whole person, so it's important for coaches not just to look 'for cognitive change, but change across the system as a whole – cognitive, emotional, physical and behavioral'. In my experience as a coach, once coachees understand the rationale for behavioural experiments, they often jump straight in to carrying them out (i.e. from the first session onwards) with their new beliefs guiding the way – creative rather than revisionist – and expect to make, and usually do, quicker progress as a result.

Table 23.1 Noting a behavioural experiment

Situation	Prediction: What do I think will happen?	Experiment based on new belief	Outcome: What happened? What did I learn?
Colleague keeps interrupting me and I keep letting him, which I want to stop.	If I tell him that he interrupts me too often, then he will get angry with me and there will be a bad atmosphere between us. I'll find this situation difficult to tolerate and I'll probably give in to him as I usually do.	I'll point out to him times I'm available for discussion, but not whenever he chooses. If there is going to be a bad atmosphere between us because of my new attitude towards him, then I'm going to start learning to cope with it without giving in to him.	He got angry, stormed off and there was a bad atmosphere between us, so the prediction was true except for me giving in. I learnt I could stand my ground, tolerate bad atmospheres and keep pointing out the same message to him. His interruptions have greatly reduced which has allowed me to get on with more of my own work.

24

Dealing with deeper beliefs

Sometimes a coachee's emotional reaction to an event can seem disproportionate, occasionally greatly so, to what actually occurred. For example, Janet, a highly regarded projects manager, presented an idea at a meeting and a colleague commented that 'It hadn't been thought through clearly enough'. Janet felt angry – 'He's insulted, demeaned me' – but didn't express it. That evening she brooded for several hours on his comment, went obsessively over her notes to try and find the weaknesses in her arguments, and only slept for a few hours. In the coaching session, Janet agreed that she'd overreacted to his comment: 'Everybody's ideas at the meetings get a going over, so why didn't I take it in my stride?' Such overreactions usually point to the presence of deeper beliefs that have been activated.

One method for uncovering these deeper beliefs is using the Downward Arrow Technique (Burns, 1999). By pursuing the personal meaning of the automatic, emotionally-charged thought (drilling down), the coach helps the coachee to reveal layers of thought until an underlying belief is located – the cognitive source of the coachee's strong emotion. Each thought uncovered is assumed to be temporarily true in the search for the belief. The rationale for the technique was explained to Janet and she gave her permission for the coach to proceed with it. Janet's automatic thought was: 'He's insulted, demeaned me.'

Coach: Let's assume that's true, what would it mean to you?

↓

Janet: He thinks that I don't know my job.

↓

Coach: And if that's true, why would that be upsetting to you?

↓

Janet: It might put doubts into people's minds that he's right.

↓

Coach: And if that's true, what would that mean to you?

↓

Janet: [visibly tense, eyes moistening] If they agree with him, then I've lost my colleagues' trust, respect and confidence in my abilities.

[An underlying assumption, 'If . . . then', has been revealed. The coachee's intense emotional response indicates this could be the belief, so the coach checks.]

↓

Coach: Is this what you're most upset about, how your colleagues will see you?

↓

Janet: No. It's more than that.

↓

Coach: What would it mean about you if you lost their trust and respect?

↓

Janet: That I'm no good. It's really upsetting to say that.

[A negative core belief has been revealed.]

Coach: Is this the central issue for you?

↓

Janet: Yes. That's it.

[The downward arrow has found its cognitive end point.]

Beck (2011: 207; emphasis in original) suggests that 'asking what a thought means *to* the [person] often elicits an intermediate belief [underlying assumption]; asking what it means *about* the [person] usually uncovers the core belief'.

There are a number of traps to avoid in carrying out the Downward Arrow Technique. These include the following.

- The coachee's replies to the reiterated question ('What would that mean to you?' or 'Why would that be upsetting to you?') should not be challenged by the coach as this stops the arrow from going down very far, e.g. 'How do you know he thinks that?'

- The coach should not ask additional questions as this will distract the coachee from the concentrated introspective focus required for the successful completion of this task, e.g. 'What does that mean to you?', 'What are you saying to yourself?', 'What's going through your mind right now?'
- The coach should not insert their own interpretations into the question, such as 'If that's true, what does it mean to you about possible failure?' This is the coach guiding the downward arrow to their predetermined cognitive destination and coachees usually, and rightly, resist this approach, e.g. 'I know what you want me say but that's not what I think'.
- If there's no emotional arousal in the coachee, then the initial automatic thought has been wrongly chosen – there's little emotional charge attached to it – and is probably not linked to the underlying belief. Or the emotional arousal has faded as the downward arrow has veered off into speculation that is not pertinent to the coachee's concerns as the coach is on autopilot, mindlessly repeating the question:

Coach: And if you do believe that you're no good, what does that mean about you?

↓

Janet: Er . . . what does that mean about me? . . . Er . . . I don't know . . . maybe I'll become permanently unemployable. Is that what you're looking for? I've already told you – I believe I'm no good. I don't know what else to say.

[These hesitations and faltering replies indicate that the coachee has disengaged from the downward arrow and is struggling to find answers to the coach's questions. She repeats the core belief which means it's time to stop the downward arrow.]

Janet said she didn't really believe the underlying assumption, 'If they agree with him, then I've lost my colleagues' trust, respect and confidence in my abilities': 'Once I've got control of myself again, I know it's ridiculous. However, the core belief has been with me since childhood and that's a different matter altogether.' Janet wanted to embark on developmental coaching which is open-ended, longer term and usually deals with fundamental personal and professional issues. She said her father was always finding fault with her and often called her 'no good'. She internalized this as the 'truth' about herself and spent her life fighting against it – 'I'll show everyone that it's not true' – by driving herself relentlessly at university to get a first (she did) and then in her career to be very successful (she was).

Her standards were impossibly high: she had to know every aspect of every complex project she was overseeing, usually several at a time, and couldn't allow any gaps in her knowledge – a standard she could never meet. Any criticism, real, implied, anticipated or imagined, would flood her mind with doubts about her abilities, distract her from the work she was engaged in and activate her 'I'm no good' belief. Keeping a note of these 'downward spirals into despair' and how long they lasted (e.g. 5, 10 or 15 minutes) often meant that several hours per week were non-productive (in her mind, this was more evidence confirming the truth of her core belief). To make up this 'lost time' as she called it, she would stay late at the office and take work home. Trying to disprove her negative core belief simply kept her focused on it; when she was criticized, this again confirmed that she would never be able to prove the belief false, no matter how hard she tried.

In coaching, the focus was on developing an alternative view of herself that was balanced and realistic. This became, in Janet's words, 'Project Bright Light'. Issues discussed included the following.

- Janet's father was not an unchallengeable authority on her character and, she said, he was an unhappy man who took out his unhappiness on her. Janet had a great interest in philosophy but, ironically, didn't follow the philosopher's dictum with regard to her father's view of her: 'Assume nothing, question everything'.
- Learning to see that judgements about aspects of her work performance, favourable or unfavourable, were not judgements about her worth as a human being – this was the connection she made: 'I'm a good person when things are going well' (self-worth rises) and 'I'm no good when I'm criticized' (self-worth plummets).

- Refraining from labelling herself because no single global label, positive or negative, could ever capture the complexity and changeability of a person, but Janet can label those aspects of her performance she wishes to improve (see Chapter 17).
- Criticism is inevitable (no one escapes it), but it doesn't have to have deeper, darker implications for Janet when she receives it. She can decide if the criticism is accurate and how she attends to address it; if it's inaccurate, state the reasons why.
- Introducing flexibility into her thinking about her harsh, unrelenting standards: high (but not impossibly high) standards are fine as long as Janet doesn't believe they are a protection against making mistakes, others finding fault or having no gaps in her knowledge.
- Collecting evidence of all the achievements in her life, which were often discredited when Janet's 'I'm no good' belief was active, underlined the new belief she wanted to adopt – 'I am very competent'.

Janet's new belief was not meant to be her essence or identity but was rooted in a more complex understanding of herself:

> *Healthy self-esteem is not about the power of positive thinking, or about encouraging you to become as unrealistically positive about yourself as you were unrealistically negative. It is about achieving a balanced, unbiased view of yourself which puts your weaknesses and flaws in the context of a broadly favourable perspective, and cheerleads for 'good enough' rather than 'perfect', allowing you to accept yourself just as you are [this acceptance doesn't preclude changing aspects of yourself].*
>
> *(Fennell, 2016: 318)*

For Janet, the key progress markers showing that she was deepening her conviction in her new belief were:

1. When she received direct criticism or it was implied by a person's behaviour towards her, she said, 'I still wobble a bit inside but most of the time I remain focused and try to be as objective as possible in dealing with it'.

2. Her 'downward spirals into despair' reduced significantly as a consequence – 'When I do have one, it lasts no more than a minute or two' – and the time reclaimed was put to productive use, such as spending more of it dealing with over 200 emails daily and going home earlier.

Coaching lasted nine months, and weekly sessions were tapered off to fortnightly and monthly as progress was made and consolidated. The coachee requested follow-up sessions for six and twelve months' time to see if her gains from coaching were holding over the longer term as she acted as her own coach.

25

Mindfulness

So far in this book on cognitive behavioural coaching (CBC), coachees have been encouraged to stand back from their upsetting or unproductive thoughts, examine them objectively and develop more helpful, goal-oriented thoughts. Another way to deal with these thoughts is to observe them without engaging with them. This non-engagement with thoughts is called mindfulness. Mindfulness is a development in cognitive behavioural therapy (CBT) that teaches individuals to observe their thoughts and feelings in the present moment without judging, controlling or attempting to change them. Upsetting thoughts can appear stronger than they actually are because we keep arguing or pleading with them, obsessing about or trying to suppress them, attempting to relax them away or exhorting ourselves to think positively – all to no avail as we've become prisoners of our thinking. Every time we engage with an upsetting belief, we give it credibility because we wouldn't be engaging with it if it didn't seem credible to us. Mindfulness teaches that accepting, not fighting against, these unpleasant inner experiences is a powerful way of reducing their adverse impact upon us; in other words, we need to change our relationship to them.

Teaching mindfulness can involve learning meditation: psychological studies have shown that, among other benefits, 'Anxiety, depression and irritability all decrease with regular sessions of meditation. Memory also improves, reaction times become faster and mental and physical stamina increase' (Williams and Penman, 2011: 6). Mindfulness detachment, which does not involve meditation, teaches individuals to see thoughts and feelings as, for example, clouds floating by, cold calls you don't respond to, or as trains entering and leaving a station without getting on one (Leahy, 2017).

The person is not expected to sit there all day observing their thoughts (just as they're not expected to challenge their upsetting thoughts all the time), but to get on with their valued activities while accepting the thoughts are still with them. Mindfulness practices can become part of a person's daily life. A striking outcome of learning mindfulness is described by the coach Max Landsberg (2015: 82) as being able 'to use the focused yet relaxed mind for intense action with rapier precision. The goal is not meditating yourself to sleep, but gathering yourself to spring . . . into effortless action'. This is the very opposite of the misconception that mindfulness teaches passivity – the person learning to put up with discontents in their life rather than using mindfulness to improve the quality of their life.

It might seem that changing and just observing thoughts are incompatible change methodologies and to mix the two would be conceptually confusing to the coachee: 'I'm not clear: is the best way to deal with these troublesome thoughts of mine to challenge and change them or leave them alone to wither on the vine?' However, the following coaching example shows both approaches being used as this was what the coachee requested. The coachee, David, was a senior manager who described his boss as 'abrasive, someone who doesn't suffer fools gladly'.

David: When he tells you something, he expects to say it only once, but sometimes he rushes it and it's difficult to catch everything he said. To ask him clarifying questions about what he's just said means you're an idiot. He's actually said that to some people. Sometimes I leave his office unclear about what I'm supposed to do and I get into my 'What if?' worry thoughts that I'm going to screw up, be humiliated, sacked, family life falls apart and it's the end of everything. I'm embarrassed to say it, but I'm such a worrier.

Coach: Something I want to clarify with you: do you ask him for further information if you don't understand what he's said to you?

David: Not usually. I have done a few times but the impatience in his voice is off-putting, so I'm not listening to what he's saying because I'm thinking, 'Am I an idiot for not getting it the first time?'

Coach: Do you believe it?

David: I don't want to, but sometimes I do. It's when I'm struggling with all the pressures of the job and I see some of my colleagues coping better than me and then he barks instructions at me which I don't fully understand and I wonder if I'm up to the job and . . .

Coach: And you conclude what?

David: Maybe I am an idiot. I want to focus on this issue as well as standing up to him but not in a confrontational way. I don't want to spend time with the 'What ifs?' as it distracts me, sometimes considerably so, from getting on with my job. And sometimes I do it at home which interferes with family life.

Coach: So, to sum up, you want to engage with the 'I'm an idiot' belief and replace it, as well as acting assertively with your boss when necessary, but disengage from the 'What ifs?' when they start.

David: That's it in a nutshell.

David embarked on an eight-week mindfulness meditation programme (with accompanying CD) as described in Williams and Penman's (2011) book. Mindfulness practice (listening to the CD) was conducted at home and, despite being busy, David said he was committed to finding the time to carrying it out. Through his meditation practice, he soon found that when the worry thoughts appeared, he focused on his breathing to ground himself in the moment, saw these thoughts as mental events, not facts, without getting entangled in them, and then returned his attention to what he'd been working on. Less and less time was spent engaging with his worry thoughts at work or home. With his 'I'm an idiot' belief, what did he want to replace it with?

David: That I'm not an idiot.

Coach: You're still focused on idiocy with that belief?

David: I'm not sure what to suggest. I'm stumped.

Coach: An alternative and balanced view would encompass your undoubted strengths, acceptance of your vulnerability when the pressure sometimes gets to you, and picking areas for performance improvement which you've already started achieving through the mindfulness meditation programme. A balanced view of oneself is a psychologically mature view in contrast to the basic, unsophisticated views I hear so often such as 'You're either strong or weak, successful or unsuccessful, intelligent or stupid, fighter or quitter' and so on.

David: Okay. That makes sense. I know I'm good at my job and I want to improve certain aspects of it, such as asking if I don't understand what my boss has said and listening to his actual reply which will make it clearer for me in terms of what I have to do. In other words, stop being intimidated by his abrasiveness. Some of my colleagues are not intimidated by it and just roll their eyes when he's in one of his moods.

Coach: Could you ask them for a few tips?

David: I will do that. I wouldn't have done it before because I was worried, 'What if they see me as weak for asking?' The unsophisticated view.

Coach: Good. You're learning.

With a much firmer conviction in his abilities, David undertook some role play in the session, with the coach playing David's abrasive boss and David rehearsing why clarification was important: 'If I don't precisely know what it is you want from me, I might give you suboptimal results which we both wouldn't want. After all, my goals support your goals which, in turn, support the company's goals. Everyone benefits.' No longer intimidated by his boss's manner and seeking clarification when necessary (sometimes accompanied by his 'My goals . . .' speech), David noticed that his boss's instructions were delivered in a slower and clearer way which benefitted both David and his colleagues. Also, David said he was going to maintain his mindfulness practice over the long term as he enjoyed feeling much calmer and more focused in his work: 'The time I spent worrying has now been reclaimed and redirected into my work.'

26

Resilience

Resilience is the bedrock of positive mental health (Persaud, 2001). Reivich and Shatté (2002: 1) emphasize that we all need resilience:

> *More than fifty years of scientific research have powerfully demonstrated that resilience is the key to success at work and satisfaction in life. Where you fall on the resilience curve – your natural reserves of resilience – affects your performance in school and at work, your physical health, your mental health, and the quality of your relationships. It is the basic ingredient to happiness and success.*

Resilience can be the framework, in both therapy and coaching, within which difficulties are discussed and resolved (Neenan, 2018). Given that everyone has some degree of resilience – it's often said that resilience is ordinary, not extraordinary (Grotberg, 2003) – the focus in coaching is usually on those areas where coachees' 'natural reserves of resilience' are depleted and there's a frustrating sense of little forward momentum, no matter what they try (see coaching example in Chapter 29). A definition of resilience I would offer is: marshalling your resources (e.g. psychological, social, spiritual) to cope adaptively with tough times and emerging from them sometimes a better, stronger, wiser person. I say 'sometimes' because the lessons learnt overcoming tough times can be forgotten once these times have passed. Some of the factors associated with resilience include the following.

- Keeping events in perspective: appraising events in a calm and measured way that enables you to distinguish between what aspects of a situation are within your control to change and which ones are not.

- Self-acceptance: refraining from rating yourself (e.g. 'I'm weak') but rating aspects of yourself such as certain beliefs and behaviours ('They're unhelpful') that hinder goal-attainment (see Chapter 17).
- Flexibility: the ability to think and act flexibly in the face of challenging and changing circumstances rather than remaining locked into a fixed mindset of how things should or shouldn't be irrespective of what the empirical reality is.
- Support from others: asking for or accepting support in your time of need. Resilience is not developed in social isolation. Positive relationships are seen as a key protective factor across the lifespan when hard times arrive (Masten and Wright, 2010).
- Self-regulation: directing your mind and behaviour to carrying out the steps required to achieve your goals and restraining the impulses that interfere with this process or threaten to undermine it, such as not making decisions based upon how you feel in the moment (e.g. comfort eating because you're upset) but how you want to feel at a later date (e.g. pleased with losing two stone).
- Curiosity: trying things out, asking questions, making discoveries to increase understanding of yourself and the world around you.
- Mindfulness: acknowledging the presence of negative thoughts and feelings without getting entangled in them – going forward despite their existence (see Chapter 25).
- Finding meaning: to guide you through dark times towards a brighter future.

Resilience has traditionally been discussed in the context of adversity, but in recent years this discussion has been expanded to teach people resilience attitudes and skills to cope with the vicissitudes of daily life (Brooks and Goldstein, 2003). Resilience is a quality sought in employees (Coutu, 2003), and career resilience (Grotberg, 2003) is required to keep adapting to a constantly changing work environment. Resilience is a subject of enduring interest to individuals, groups and organizations. Resilience training and cognitive behavioural coaching (CBC) make a very good fit as they both start from the same position: revealing a person's attitudes to adverse events explains their emotional and behavioural reactions to them (Reivich and Shatté, 2002).

The quickest way to discover if a person is 'struggling well' – Higgin's (1994) wonderfully pithy description of resilience – is to reveal their attitudes to coping with adversity (e.g. 'This situation is not going to beat me'). However, a snapshot taken at a particular moment of their 'struggling well' progress does not guarantee an accurate prediction of its outcome as they might give up if they encounter too many setbacks. Conversely, someone struggling poorly might eventually receive some unexpected social support which enables them to achieve a favourable outcome to their troubles. So the meaning, helpful or unhelpful, we attach to events is not static and therefore can change over time.

An unhelpful idea about resilience is that hard times have tempered the steel of a person's character and it will never break, whatever life throws at them. No matter how robust they've become, they still remain vulnerable to coping poorly with future adversities. Resilience shouldn't be seen as a fixed personality trait so that the person will demonstrate it in all adverse situations rather than in some but not others (Masten and Wright, 2010). A forceful, no-nonsense manager I was doing some performance coaching with was involved in a car accident. He needed some time off work to deal with his injuries as well as the shock, but the real shock for him was not being able to get back to work within a couple of days.

As Dryden (2017) points out, when adversities happen during the course of coaching, is the coachee too disturbed to deal with it in the context of coaching and so requires a referral to a therapist? Alternatively, does the coach have a psychological model, such as being originally trained in cognitive behaviour therapy (CBT), with which to deal with their coachee's disturbance? In this case, the coachee, Richard, wanted to discuss his angry and perplexing response to the car crash, and performance coaching was put off until a later date (though it quickly became clear that unrealistic standards of 'How I must be and be seen' were at the heart of all his difficulties). The coaching sessions were now conducted on Skype instead of face-to-face.

Richard: I can't understand why I'm not back at work. It's frustrating being at home, weak and pathetic about the crash. It seems as if I'm losing control of myself. Incredible.

Coach: Some might say that you're showing a normal human response to the accident by needing a recovery period.

Richard: My normal human response is to be back at work *now*.

Coach: What does your doctor say?

Richard: Probably another two weeks off work.

Coach: Why does being off work mean you're weak and pathetic?

Richard: I always bounce back from whatever the situation is.

Coach: Is that your ideal resilience response?

Richard: My ideal and actual response.

Coach: Until now.

Richard: Yes, until now.

Coach: How are your resilience skills helping you to cope in this situation?

Richard: Not too well it seems. Look, if you've got some ideas about this situation, give them to me instead of keep asking me questions. Give me some meat to chew on.

[The coachee is not interested in responding to questions, so the coach moves into didactic mode, but not completely.]

Coach: Okay. Your definition of resilience is part of the problem, 'I always bounce back from whatever the situation is', because you're not bouncing back in this situation and you don't know how to cope with it apart from keep demanding you should be back at work. So, you're stuck at home with your anger and . . . how do you feel when you say you're 'weak and pathetic'? Another question I'm afraid.

Richard: If I'm honest, somewhat ashamed.

Coach: Stuck at home with anger and shame. Now, one of the central features of resilience is adapting your thinking and behaviour to cope constructively with whatever situation you find yourself in . . .

Richard: Which presumably I'm not doing . . .

Coach: Correct. So, unfortunately, at the present time you're acting non-resiliently. No one acts resiliently at all times under all circumstances but the question for you is: how long do you want to continue to act non-resiliently in this situation?

Richard: I want to stop acting non-resiliently. Give me some more ideas.

Coach: Structure your day with some interesting activities.

Richard: That's what my wife says instead of moaning all day long.

Coach: Then follow her good advice. I will suggest some reading on resilience that provides a more detailed and accurate account of resilience instead of the popular, feel-good, effortless bouncing back image that many people subscribe to. I've seen lot of executives, like you, who see themselves as weak and feel ashamed if they're not bouncing back from every difficulty they face. Self-condemnation is not part of a resilient outlook; what is part of it is extracting some useful lessons from the experience that leads to personal and professional development. I use the term 'coming back' in my coaching work, not 'bouncing back', which means there are different speeds and pathways to recovery from adversity and you don't link your self-worth to how fast or slowly your recovering.

Richard: You've given me a lot to think about and do. I'd better get on with it then.

The suggested reading was *Coping with Life's Challenges* (Dryden, 2010) and *Developing Resilience* (Neenan, 2018). From this reading and further discussions in the coaching sessions, Richard came to some sobering conclusions:

- Another shock for Richard was how his self-worth was so closely tied to his workplace performance and his forceful, no-nonsense public persona – any slippage in these areas was a sign of weakness which he dreaded in himself and feared others judging him as such (which was why he was desperate to get back to work to show these others that 'nothing can keep me down'). He was too hard on himself as well as the people he managed.
- Looking back, Richard admitted he didn't bounce back all the time from his difficulties – the bouncing back bravado was meant to impress others.

- Richard's superman view of being resilient kept him trapped in a cycle of non-learning: when he didn't respond to difficulties in the way he demanded of himself, he engaged in what he saw as 'motivational' harsh self-criticism so it wouldn't happen again (which, of course, it did). He started showing himself some compassion, understanding that the fault was in his rigid and unrealistic standards and these standards needed to be modified if genuine progress was to be made when he fell short in some way.

When Richard went back to work, the coaching focus on coping constructively with adversity began to change (at his request) to longer-term developmental coaching. He eventually reformulated his rigid standards into flexible and compassionate ones: 'I'm strong and capable, but also vulnerable at times. When these vulnerabilities occur, I will seek to understand and improve my behaviour, not condemn myself for it.' With this softening of his attitude towards himself, Richard took a more helpful, much less condemnatory stance to those of his direct reports he'd previously dismissed as 'losers' when they complained of heavy workloads or sometimes missed performance targets; in other words, when they fell short.

27

The end of coaching and beyond

The end of coaching is often discussed at its outset: by working with the coach, the coachee will learn a range of self-help skills to use both in and between the sessions in order to become their own coach, and will terminate coaching in that capacity. Endings in cognitive behavioural coaching (CBC) are usually straightforward if certain conditions have been met:

- The coachee has accepted the principle and practice of psychological responsibility.
- The goals are clear and measurable and within the coachee's control to achieve.
- Regular monitoring of progress towards those goals through the implementation of the coachee's action plan.
- The relationship is based on collaboration and regular feedback and summaries are sought from the coachee to determine if any difficulties or misunderstandings have arisen.
- Any impasses in coaching are addressed and ruptures in the relationship are repaired.

The coachee can be asked to summarize any valuable lessons they learnt in coaching:

Coachee: Three things really stand out for me. First, I like this idea of stepping back to examine my thinking more objectively rather than accepting my thoughts as correct when I'm upset, such as 'Criticism means I'm crap'. Second, widening my perspective to see what other options are available to help me solve my problems. As you know, I was a black or white thinker so options for me were either this one or that one, nothing else. Third, I really like the behavioural experiments to test out ideas rather than remain stuck with them. I've been doing these experiments outside of work as well.

Coach: Can you give an example of an experiment outside of work?

Coachee: I've started on a DIY car maintenance course.

Coach: What's the idea you're testing?

Coachee: The old-fashioned one that as I'm a woman I won't be able to understand car engines like a man naturally would. The idea turned out to be nonsense. I'm really enjoying it and making good progress.

Coach: Glad to hear it. On another issue, how do you propose to maintain your gains from coaching so they serve you over the long term rather than possibly fading away in the next few weeks or months through inaction? As they say, use them [CBC skills] or lose them.

Coachee: As I said, I really like those behavioural experiments and want to do at least one a week. My husband said the other night shall we go to a Vietnamese restaurant and I said, 'Okay, I'll try it'. The food wasn't too bad. When he asked me several months ago, I said no because I was convinced I wouldn't like the food. So, 'I'll try it', is now my watchword.

Coach: Lastly, some people like to have follow-up sessions to report on their progress. Would you like one?

Coachee: I'd like one in six months. If I run into any difficulties that I'm really struggling with, can I contact you before then?

Coach: Sure you can.

Occasionally, when a coachee has reached the end of their agreed number of sessions and, by their own estimation, has made good progress in achieving some of their goals, they nevertheless may harbour some doubts about actually leaving coaching, such as 'We haven't addressed all my issues'. Coaching wasn't intended to do this and the coachee's newly-learnt CBC skills can be applied to these other issues when they've left coaching. To have resolved all their issues before they leave undermines the idea of becoming their own coach and, if the coach agrees to their request, risks the coachee becoming dependent on the coach to do all their problem solving for them; or, at the very least, relying on the coach's verbal prompts to point them in the right direction when they're unsure about what to do in a specific situation instead of them tolerating uncertainty by trying out different behavioural responses until they find the most productive one.

It's important to state that becoming one's own coach doesn't carry the imprint of finality, that is, the individual now has to sort out all their difficulties without any further recourse to CBC. Individuals can come back to coaching when they want to, and some of my coachees treat me as a continuing professional resource they consult from time to time.

Another issue to deal with in the last session is the possibility of a setback or relapse. A setback is a check in the coachee's progress whereas a relapse is a return to the problems the coachee originally presented with. Setbacks are inevitable in the post-coaching progress of fallible human beings, but a setback doesn't have to turn into a relapse – no slippery slope inevitability:

Typically, slippery slope arguments obscure the fact that in most cases we can decide how far down a slope we want to go: we can dig our heels in at a certain point and say 'here and no further' . . . The metaphor of slipperiness with its connotations of inevitable descent and frightening loss of control does not seem to allow this possibility. It conjures up images of powerlessness which may be inappropriate to the case in question.

(Warburton, 2007: 132)

For example, a person may start overeating again because they blame stress at work and believe they can't stop until work stress eases ('I'm really worried about all this weight I'm putting on. I don't want to return to my previous weight but what can I do with all this work piling up on my desk?'). In fact, they've given themself permission to continue overeating rather than saying 'here and no further', in other words, taking personal responsibility for re-establishing self-control. Even though the person may believe it, they're not actually in the grip of a compulsion to eat but it's certainly harder to exercise self-control than it is to surrender to their perceived need for immediate pleasure. So, from the top to the bottom of the slope there are a number of decision points. This means the person can give themself permission to continue with their self-defeating behaviour (relapse approaches) or withhold permission in order to stop it. No experience has to be wasted if the person is prepared to learn from it, so relapse can prove instructive. Leahy (2017) suggests two lessons:

1. The person can see the relapse as a natural experiment – what happens when they *don't* follow the guidelines for continuing progress.
2. Seeing the relapse as a productive type of pain – it alerts the person to what isn't working in their life and to take corrective steps in their thinking and behaviour.

Coachees need to remember that setbacks and relapses are incidents in the course of one's progress, not its whole story, which some discouraged coachees can come to believe.

28

Supervision

There is usually a gap (perhaps inevitably so) between what a coach (or therapist) says goes on in the session and what actually occurs within it. Supervision, using audio and/or video recordings of some sessions, can demonstrate how wide or narrow this gap is. Just relying on the coach's account of what went on, including their effort to be as objective as possible, remains a one-sided view and it's this account the supervisor has to work with. Listening to or watching a session or, more usually, an excerpt from it, widens considerably the scope of the discussion in supervision and can pinpoint difficulties in the coach's practice that they may not be aware of. Equally, the recording may show a higher level of competence in contrast to the somewhat gloomy ('It's not very good'), pre-listening description often delivered by the supervisee.

Supervision 'is an essential and central component of both CBT [cognitive behavioural therapy] training and professional practice post-qualification' (Branch and Dryden, 2012: 439). Supervision, including recordings of sessions, is a requirement for a cognitive behavioural therapist's accreditation and subsequent reaccreditations with the BABCP (British Association for Behavioural and Cognitive Psychotherapies). With regard to supervision in cognitive behavioural coaching (CBC), Professor Stephen Palmer, one of the UK's leading CBC coaches, says: 'CBC courses stress the need for regular supervision during training and post-qualification. It is recommended that audio recordings of coaching sessions are used occasionally to aid the supervisory process although this is not mandatory. This reflects how the coaching field has developed from different roots compared to counselling and therapy' (personal communication, 2 June 2017).

I recommend to my coaching supervisees to record their sessions regularly so that between a third to half of our supervision sessions will contain excerpts from their audio recordings. I point out to my supervisees that I can't give them my best supervisory efforts if I don't know what's going on in the session and I want more than a snapshot (or audioshot) of a session: I want to see how coaching unfolds over time. Why is supervision important? For the following reasons.

- To monitor the quality of the CBC service being provided to the coachee. For example, are the techniques and strategies being used by the coach the right or most helpful ones to assist the coachee achieve their goals? Is the coach encouraging collaborative empiricism or taking a unilateral 'I know best' stance in decision making? Does the coach respond non-defensively to criticism from the coachee or react with a barely suppressed irritability? Is the coachee talking and telling too much – a frequent occurrence – rather than advancing the session through Socratic questioning?

- Helping to improve coaches' existing skills like agenda-setting, or acquiring new ones such as turning coachees' rhetorical questions into clear, unambiguous statements (see Chapter 13).

- Changing unproductive attitudes (e.g. 'I must never say "I don't know" as this shows incompetence. If I have to dispense a little bullshit now and again to cover my lack of knowledge, so be it') and behaviours, such as presenting the same persona – always upbeat and relentlessly positive – to all coachees rather than adapting themself to the coachee's preferred interpersonal style.

- Pinpointing coaches' beliefs and behaviours that interfere with their professional development as well as their coachees' progress. For example, whenever the coachee brings up a sensitive issue and says 'I don't feel comfortable discussing it', the coach keeps replying, 'That's okay, we can discuss it later in the session or in another session'. CBC, like CBT, is not a discomfort-free zone, though the coach tries to make it one with their 'discuss it later' strategy because they believe: 'If I encourage the coachee to talk about it now, she might get upset with me, think I'm an insensitive, incompetent coach and complain to others about me which might adversely affect my business.' Embracing discomfort is an inevitable part of the change process, which will have benefits for both coach and coachee.

- Reminds coaches that no matter how many years they've been practising, they will never reach a position where their experience has inoculated them against making any further mistakes, where their blind spots and vulnerabilities have been removed, or where their thinking is always rational and there's nothing else to learn. They still need the critical thinking of others to examine their work (I have peer supervision).

It's worth noting that some commentators, focused on mental health services, question the assumptions that practitioners get better with experience and that supervision produces more effective practitioners. They say there's little scientific support to buttress these assumptions (Bickman, 2008). Hanna (2002: 289) speculates that perhaps 'the lack of wisdom is at the core of the puzzle concerning why the number of years of therapy experience does not seem to influence effectiveness'. Years of experience, whether as a practitioner or supervisor, are not automatically converted into wisdom, maybe just wishful thinking that this conversion has occurred. I'm sure these concerns apply equally to coaching.

Supervision can be conducted face-to-face: the supervisor is more experienced than the supervisee; or as peers with a similar level of experience; or in a group led by an experienced supervisor; or the supervisees learning from each other as no one is purported to be more experienced than the other. As well as face-to-face, supervision can be carried out over the phone or on Skype, supplemented by audio recordings of sessions which the supervisor can download and listen to prior to the supervision session. A contract can be drawn up stating what the goals of supervision are, fees, and frequency and duration of sessions. A trial period of supervision is worth considering as issues of incompatibility may arise, for instance, the supervisor as expert much prefers the supervisee to follow their instructions but the supervisee wants more discussion about their instructions and doesn't like being talked down to.

Coachees' permission to record sessions must be sought and no pressure should be brought to bear on them if they refuse. The purpose of the recording and what will be done with it after the supervision session (deleted) is explained. Over the years as a supervisor of both therapists and coaches, I've heard the same protest from many supervisees about recording: clients will be inhibited from speaking frankly and freely about their difficulties because of the presence of the recording devices. Once clients have given their permission for recording, they usually have no problems with it. It's the supervisees who are much more likely to be inhibited by the recording of sessions because it activates their central fear of being exposed in supervision as incompetent. For some, this fear follows them throughout their career: from the dread of submitting 'shockingly bad' recordings in training to years after post-qualification when they're still apprehensive that mistakes will be found in their latest supervision submission, as if they should be free of these by now.

Supervisees should prepare themselves for supervision by reflecting on their work and pinpointing the issues for discussion. If presenting an excerpt of a recording, what specific aspects of it does the supervisee want to focus on? For example: 'He keeps answering his phone in the session. You'll hear me say it's okay but it isn't really. How do I deal with this as I find him quite intimidating in a number of ways?' A coachee who presents an audio recording and says, 'Have a listen and see what you think', has a vague, somewhat lazy approach to pre-supervision preparation.

How do you find a supervisor? By looking at a professional coaching body's list of accredited supervisors (though accreditation doesn't guarantee competence), word-of-mouth recommendation, or by trying someone whose coaching work you respect. Over the years I've frequently been asked, how do you know if the person is a really good supervisor? Based on my own past experiences of trying to find such a supervisor, here are a few observations.

- You ask questions and expect clear answers but get waffle, evasiveness, jargon, clichés, formulaic responses. The person was trying to sound authoritative but without saying anything substantive. I kept thinking, 'You can't answer the question because you don't really know'. It wasn't just one question but a series of them they waffled over. They liked the title of supervisor without the requisite knowledge and experience that went with it;

- Someone who treats you as an audience to applaud their 'brilliance' as a supervisor, e.g. 'So many of my supervisees can't believe the success they're having with their clients since I became their supervisor';

- A supervisor who just repeats what's in the textbook as if they're on automatic pilot without much hope of improving their supervisory skills if they continue in this way. I wasn't going to keep paying someone who told me what I already knew – I wanted more than just the textbook; and that was

- Wisdom: the distillation of the supervisor's knowledge, understanding and experience into sound judgements that could be relied upon in dealing with the difficulties I faced with my clients. How was I to know if they were dispensing genuine wisdom or just appearing to? Quite simply because more often than not their judgements and recommendations resulted in improved outcomes for most of my clients and improvements in my skills – the whole point of supervision. I know the concept of wisdom can sound vague or mystical but the essence of it for me is the ability to cut to the core of a particular issue and see what needs to be done to resolve it.

As Hall (2010: 8) observes: 'All of us have an intuitive sense of what wisdom means and what constitutes wise behavior. In a rough, nonacademic sense . . . we know it when we see it, even if we can't define it.' Also, as frequently pointed out, being intelligent is not equivalent to being wise, so don't be overawed if a person lists all their academic qualifications to demonstrate that wisdom has been conferred on them – they still need a try-out so you can assess their skills as a possible supervisor.

I'm certainly not claiming the supervisor was unerringly wise on every issue I presented to them. Wisdom can, over time, turn unobtrusively into platitudes. As the philosopher Julian Baggini observes, wisdom is a process, not a product: 'To be wise is not to achieve a state of maturity from which one never regresses, but to keep one's understanding sharp by persisting in a habit of constant questioning and a refusal to take things for granted' (2009: 200). So, be on the alert for the possibility of your supervisor's wisdom turning into woolly thinking at some point.

29

A coaching session

I want to present a lengthy excerpt from a coaching session explaining what I'm doing and why I'm doing it. My annotations will be in square brackets. Obviously, these annotations are not meant to be definitive, just my approach to tackling the coachee's difficulties, which you may find helpful. I've removed the verbal clutter of rambling, humming and hawing, and going off at tangents. The coachee, Sandra, was a schoolteacher and head of department. She said she wasn't 'dealing very well' with a teacher in her department who was often rude to colleagues, and argumentative and obstructive at departmental meetings when Sandra brought up changes she wanted to make. Sandra's colleagues were unhappy that she was making no progress in curbing his unpleasant behaviour.

Coach: What would dealing very well with him look like?

[Does she have a vision of what she wants to achieve in coaching?]

Sandra: I want to convey a clear and consistent message regarding the changes in his behaviour that I want to see.

Coach: And if he doesn't respond to this clear and consistent message?

Sandra: Then I'll have to consider disciplinary procedures but I very much hope it doesn't come to that.

Coach: What stops you presently from conveying this clear and consistent message?

['What stops or prevents you . . .' is a key assessment question.]

Sandra: I tried to but he doesn't really pay attention.

Coach: He doesn't have to pay attention, but what stops you from being consistent and persistent in spelling out the consequences for him if he doesn't pay attention and change his behaviour?

[The coach still hasn't got an answer to his question.]

Sandra: Putting it like that makes me sound harsh.

Coach: Does that conflict with your self-image?

[Suggesting a hypothesis for her inaction.]

Sandra: I like to be seen by people as supportive, not punitive. I don't like people to think badly of me. I suppose it does hold me back from getting to grips with this situation. I don't like confrontation and the bad feelings that go with it.

[She has identified a psychological block to progress.]

Coach: Have you had any confrontations with him?

Sandra: Not yet, but he gets moody when I bring up the subject of his behaviour.

Coach: What's the problem with confrontation if it gets to that stage?

Sandra: I might crumble in the face of his anger and I'll lose my authority with him.

Coach: What authority do you have with him at the moment?

[She's assuming having something that might already be lost.]

Sandra: Little, I expect.

Coach: You told me earlier that the other teachers are pressing you to do something about his behaviour as you're head of department, it's your responsibility. They're fed up with him. Are you being seen by them as supportive of their needs?

[Pointing out the discrepancy between Sandra wanting to be seen as supportive and others feeling unsupported by her present inaction.]

Sandra: No. They're also getting fed up with my faffing around with him.

Coach: And your authority with them?

Sandra: Not very impressive at the present time. It's all so frustrating: I want to do the right thing but it's turning out badly.

Coach: You're doing the wrong 'right thing' and that's why it's turning out badly.

[The coach is being deliberately enigmatic to get her undivided attention.]

Sandra: You've lost me there. What do you mean?

Coach: The right thing for you is how you want to be seen – supportive, not punitive – rather than focusing on what's required of you as head of department which is firm action. You're putting your personal needs before your professional duties.

Sandra: That's harsh . . . but unfortunately true. Let me ask you a question: do you think you're being supportive of me with this problem?

Coach: I do. Your way is clearly not working in this situation. Now imagine, like you with that teacher, I'm more concerned with you seeing me as supportive and I don't want you to think badly of me. Instead of saying what I really think which might be helpful, I'm being very careful not to upset you. So you're paying me to help you find solutions but what you don't realize is that my primary concern is to be seen in the right way by you. So my personal needs would come before giving you my best efforts at problem solving. Is that want you want?

[The coach is expressing clear opinions, not faffing around with her.]

Sandra: No. If that was the case then I wouldn't be making any progress in coaching either. It's a bit of mess, isn't it?

Coach: What do you do with a mess?

Sandra: Start clearing it up. Okay. I need him to start changing his behaviour.

[Clearing up the mess starts with her, not him.]

Coach: I said, 'What do *you* need to start doing?' You're the primary problem, not him.

Sandra: Sorting out this not wanting people to think badly of me belief.

Coach: And how do you go about sorting it out?

Sandra: Well, I'm sure some of my colleagues are currently think-ing badly of me because of my inaction on this issue, so my belief is not doing what it's supposed to do. So I need a get-on-with-it belief.

Coach: And how would that sound?

Sandra: As we discussed, my professional responsibilities should and will overrule my personal needs in my dealings with him.

Coach: So how will you translate that determination into action?

[Developing an action plan.]

Sandra: I will arrange another meeting with him. This Thursday afternoon.

[The first step in the action plan.]

Coach: What's the purpose of the meeting?

Sandra: To bring up the concerns about his behaviour, what behaviour changes I want to see within a relatively short time-scale, what support I can provide in this process and what will happen if these changes don't occur.

Coach: Can you foresee any difficulties in carrying out this task?

[Troubleshooting.]

Sandra: Me. I might lose my nerve if he starts getting confrontational. How would I handle that?

Coach: You point out to him that's precisely the reason you're having this meeting, his unacceptable behaviour. Your tone needs to be formal, but don't become confrontational yourself. Once the message has been delivered, the meeting is over – it's not up for discussion.

Sandra: What about if he apologizes for his behaviour at the meeting? He always apologizes.

Coach: What happened with his previous apologies?

[The coach has given her some advice regarding the first difficulty but wants her to make an effort at troubleshooting rather than doing all the thinking for her.]

Sandra: They didn't last long. He reverted after a couple of days. So accept his apology but insist on the behaviour change which needs to be maintained which I didn't do before. When he apologized I felt sorry for him and got distracted from what I had to do.

Coach: When you speak to him at the meeting, maintain a non-distractible focus. Any more difficulties?

Sandra: I could bring up more which would all be about letting myself get sidetracked at the meeting, but the answer for each one is in the non-distractible focus. Thinking about it now, today is Monday so why am I waiting till Thursday? I'll schedule the meeting for tomorrow. You know, I'm feeling somewhat angry with myself for being pathetic about all this.

Coach: We could discuss that at the next session as this one is drawing to a close, but let's stay with the meeting. What could you do constructively with that anger?

[The coach wants to maintain the focus on action and how her anger could be deployed in this context rather than explore how she feels and possibly dissipate the momentum for change that's building within her.]

Sandra: I can use it as a motivating force to carry through what needs to be done. Obviously, I'm not going to get angry with him.

Coach: Good. In these last few minutes, any comments about the session?

[Asking for end-of-session feedback.]

Sandra: Yes. You've been clear and consistent with me about what I need to do and I want to be that way with him tomorrow. I was surprised that the focus was on me, not him. I thought at the beginning of the session we were going to discuss him and you would provide me with some insights and techniques to deal with him, but you've been dealing with me instead.

Coach: You're my client, he's not. You're the one with the psychological block, so progress won't be made until we deal with it. Self-management first, then you can turn your focus to the management of others.

Sandra: I see that now. That's a useful phrase to remember in dealing with other interpersonal issues in my department.

The meeting went ahead. In the next session Sandra said: 'I was distracted a couple of times when he began as usual to apologize but I stuck to my guns and this time he got the message.' Within the space of three meetings he was complying with the requested behaviour changes and disciplinary proceedings never became an actual issue. Though Sandra still preferred others not to think badly of her, this mindset no longer dominated her interpersonal relationships within the department: 'If difficulties have to be faced, my professional responsibilities come first, no longer my personal needs.'

30

CBC is not for everyone and how it can be improved for others

One major reason why cognitive behavioural coaching (CBC) doesn't work for some coachees is their reluctance or, at times, downright refusal to take responsibility for their thoughts, feelings and actions and, instead, blame others or the company culture for their reactions to events. Typical responses include, 'If you worked there, which you don't, then you would feel the same way too' and 'You don't understand the world of business'. They talk as if their mind is a blank slate upon which the company inscribes its values and philosophy, thereby removing their freedom of thought about the company culture/business world and how to respond to it.

Providing explanations that the human mind doesn't respond passively to events but is continually attaching meaning to them, and meaning changes over time (i.e. your viewpoint alters), can fall on deaf ears (some coachees grudgingly concede that their attitudes may not be the most helpful in dealing with the situations they're facing and at this point will give the CBC model a try). For others who see the model as having no explanatory power for them (more like explanatory impotence, e.g. 'Your approach can't help me with the boss I've got'), it's important for the coach not to get into a power struggle by trying to make the coachee accept psychological responsibility.

If a coach does get into a power struggle with a coachee, this usually means their professional self-esteem is riding on the outcome. Also, the coach will probably not realize that they're reinforcing the coachee's belief that they have no freedom of thought in coaching either. If the coachee is not interested in CBC, the coach should bring it to an end instead of persisting unproductively.

Other coachees might accept psychological responsibility but don't proceed to the next step of implementing an action plan for change or, if implemented, this is done half-heartedly or haphazardly. One of the key reasons for this half-heartedness is the coachee's belief that insight alone is sufficient to promote change – but insight needs to be coupled with action. Whatever term is used – acknowledgement, insight, awareness, understanding, enlightenment – relating to the crucial role our beliefs play in shaping our responses to events, it's not enough in itself to bring about change or, more precisely, deep and lasting change. Awareness of the thinking that lies behind an unproductive behaviour or unpleasant feeling appears to be the precursor to change, but several days or weeks later this awareness is not so motivating as the coachee reflects unenthusiastically on the effort required to change this behaviour or feeling.

If the coachee believes that insight alone will achieve their desired changes, this could be viewed as an experiment: leave coaching to see if it works; if it doesn't, they could return to restart the other kind of work they previously baulked at doing. If they do return, they need to learn the vital importance of acting consistently and persistently in support of their newly-developed productive beliefs if they hope to realize the changes they want.

With a few coachees, it becomes evident that they have significant psychological problems which require the services of a therapist, not a coach, for example, clinical depression although the initial presentation in coaching was a smiling 'I'm-looking-forward-to-working-with-you-and-achieving-good-things' upbeat approach. In other cases, some individuals view coaching as a sanitized form of therapy (i.e. the negative connotations of seeking therapy don't apply when coming to coaching), but the cognitive behavioural coach needs to be shrewd enough to know when therapy is the right arena for these coachees (Buckley and Buckley, 2006).

For some coachees, examining their thinking is an intrusive, intimate, difficult, dull or unfamiliar activity which they don't wish to undertake – they minimize the first 'c' in 'CBC'. They prefer to try out different behaviours to achieve their desired outcomes – cBC – and they don't mind offering their thoughts on the successes and setbacks in pursuing their chosen behavioural options, but no self-focus. The coach should respect this preference and not see it as a psychological block which needs to be addressed. The actual block might be within them if they dogmatically insist, 'We always examine thoughts and beliefs in CBC. That's what we're supposed to do'.

Other coachees might see questioning specific beliefs as a kind of doubt virus that could spread through their entire belief system – a settled worldview being upended. If this is the case, the coach could suggest that a few small experiments in specific areas could be conducted (as a prelude to examining more troubling beliefs) by going against an ingrained habit – 'I always read my newspaper on the train to work' – to see if not doing it for a week starts tremors throughout the coachee's belief system.

In my experience, it's not usually the outright rejection of CBC that's the problem but how it's presented and implemented. For example, I've supervised coaches where I've heard them say on DVRs (digital voice recordings) of sessions that 'It's all to do with your unhelpful thinking in these situations', thereby shutting down emotional expression by implying that it clutters up the coaching process, problems are decontextualized (i.e. only created in your head and adverse circumstances have no role to play in the person's difficulties), and giving the impression that CBC is a dry-as-dust cerebral exchange of unhelpful ideas for helpful ones. Also, some coaches desperate to make a good impression, particularly on executives, convince themselves that they have to act as a fast-paced incisive questioner thereby shrinking the coachee's reflective space to consider their replies. Allied to this fast-paced style is having all the (well-rehearsed) answers to show how wise and experienced the coach is, and the coachee's role is to show their appreciation of this 'wise mind' in the comments they make.

Many difficulties in coaching can be minimized or avoided if the coach remembers to obtain frequent feedback from the coachee in order to make adjustments to the coaching journey and relationship. Often, assumptions made by the coach are not shared with the coachee, thereby undermining the coach's claim that 'ideas need to be tested', and these untested assumptions can lead to wrong turnings being taken in coaching. I often suggest to the coaches I supervise that when they don't test their assumptions, they should make a tick on a piece of paper they carry with them, and at the end of the day or week count how many ticks they've accumulated. They're often surprised or shocked by how many ticks there are. So, don't assume, ask!

Appendix

For information on cognitive behavioural coaching courses contact:

Centre for Coaching
156 Westcombe Hill
London SE3 7DH
www.centreforcoaching.com
Tel: 0845 680 2065
The centre offers certificate and diploma courses. The director of training is Professor Stephen Palmer.

For information on cognitive behavioural therapy contact:

British Association for Behavioural & Cognitive Psychotherapies (BABCP)
Imperial House
Hornby Street
Bury
Lancashire BL9 5BN
www.babcp.com
Tel: 0161 705 4304

References

Arkowitz, H. and Lilienfeld, S. O. (2017) *Facts and Fictions in Mental Health*. Chichester: Wiley.

Arnold, J., Cooper, C. L. and Robertson, I. T. (1995) *Work Psychology: Understanding Human Behaviour in the Workplace*, 2nd edn. London: Pitman.

Baggini, J. (2009) *Should You Judge This Book By Its Cover? 100 Fresh Takes on Familiar Sayings and Quotations*. London: Granta.

Beck, A. T. (1976) *Cognitive Therapy and the Emotional Disorders*. New York: New American Library.

Beck, A. T. (1987) Cognitive models of depression, in *Journal of Cognitive Psychotherapy*, 1 (1): 5–37.

Beck, A. T., Emery, G. and Greenberg, R. L. (1985) *Anxiety Disorders and Phobias: A Cognitive Perspective*. New York: Guilford.

Beck, A. T., Rush, A. J., Shaw, B. F. and Emery, G. (1979) *Cognitive Therapy of Depression*. New York: Guilford.

Beck, J. S. (2011) *Cognitive Behavior Therapy: Basics and Beyond*, 2nd edn. New York: Guilford.

Bickman, L. (2008) Practice makes perfect and other myths about mental health services, in S. O. Lilienfeld, J. Ruscio and S. J. Lynn (eds) *Navigating the Mindfield: A Guide to Separating Science from Pseudoscience in Mental Health*. New York: Prometheus.

Blackburn, S. (2016) *Oxford Dictionary of Philosophy*, 3rd edn. Oxford: Oxford University Press.

Branch, R. and Dryden, W. (2012) Supervision of CBT therapists, in W. Dryden and R. Branch (eds) *The CBT Handbook*. London: Sage.

Brooks, R. and Goldstein, S. (2003) *The Power of Resilience: Achieving Balance, Confidence, and Personal Strength in Your Life*. New York: McGraw-Hill.

Buckley, A. and Buckley, C. (2006) *A Guide to Coaching and Mental Health*. Hove: Routledge.

Burns, D. D. (1999) *Feeling Good: The New Mood Therapy*, 2nd edn. New York: Avon.

Butler, G., Fennell, M. and Hackmann, A. (2008) *Cognitive-Behavioral Therapy for Anxiety Disorders: Mastering Clinical Challenges*. New York: Guilford.

Clark, D. A. (1995) Perceived limitations of standard cognitive therapy: a consideration of efforts to revise Beck's theory and therapy, *Journal of Cognitive Psychotherapy*, 9 (3): 153–172.

Clark, D. A. and Beck, A. T. (2010) *Cognitive Therapy of Anxiety Disorders*. New York: Guilford.

Clark, D. A. and Steer, R. A. (1996) Empirical status of the cognitive model of anxiety and depression, in P. M. Salkovskis (ed.) *Frontiers of Cognitive Therapy*. New York: Guilford.

Coutu (2003) How resilience works, in *Harvard Business Review on Building Personal and Organizational Resilience*. Boston, MA: Harvard Business School Press.

DiGiuseppe, R. (1991) Comprehensive cognitive disputing in RET, in M. E. Bernard (ed.) *Using Rational-Emotive Therapy Effectively: A Practitioner's Guide*. New York: Plenum.

Dobson, D. and Dobson, K. S. (2009) *Evidence-Based Practice of Cognitive-Behavioral Therapy*. New York: Guilford.

Dryden, W. (2010) *Coping with Life's Challenges: Moving on from Adversity*. London: Sheldon.

Dryden, W. (2011) *Dealing with Clients' Emotional Problems in Life Coaching*. Hove: Routledge.

Dryden, W. (2017) *Very Brief Cognitive Behavioural Coaching (VBCBC)*. Abingdon: Routledge.

Dryden, W. and Neenan, M. (2015) *Rational Emotive Behaviour Therapy: 100 Key Points and Techniques*, 2nd edn. Hove: Routledge.

Edgerton, N. and Palmer, S. (2005) SPACE: a psychological model for use within cognitive behavioural coaching, therapy and stress management, *The Coaching Psychologist* 2 (2): 25–31.

Ellis, A. (2002) *Overcoming Resistance: A Rational Emotive Behavior Therapy Integrated Approach*, 2nd edn. New York: Springer.

Ellis, A. and MacLaren, C. (1998) *Rational Emotive Behavior Therapy: A Therapist's Guide*. Atascadero, CA: Impact.

Fennell, M. (2016) *Overcoming Low Self-Esteem: A Self-Help Guide Using Cognitive Behavioural Techniques*, 2nd edn. Robinson: London.

Frankl, V. (1946/1985) *Man's Search for Meaning* (revised and updated). New York: Washington Square Press.

Furnham, A. (2012) *The Talented Manager: 67 Gems of Business Wisdom*. New York: Palgrave Macmillan.

Grant, A. M. (2009) Coach or couch? *Harvard Business Review*, 87 (1): 97.

Grant, A. M. (2012) Foreword, in M. Neenan and S. Palmer (eds) *Cognitive Behavioural Coaching in Practice: An Evidence Based Approach*. Hove: Routledge.

Greene, J. and Grant, A. M. (2003) *Solution-Focused Coaching: Managing People in a Complex World*. London: Momentum.

Grieger, R. (2017) *Developing Unrelenting Drive, Dedication, and Determination: A Cognitive Behavior Workbook*. New York: Routledge.

Grotberg, E. H. (2003) What is resilience? How do you promote it? How do you use it?, in E. H. Grotberg (ed.) *Resilience for Today: Gaining Strength from Adversity*. Westport, CT: Praeger.

Hall, S. S. (2010) *Wisdom: From Philosophy to Neuroscience*. New York: Knopf.

Hanna, F. J. (2002) *Therapy with Difficult Clients: Using the Precursors Model to Awaken Change*. Washington, DC: American Psychological Association.

Hauck, P. (1980) *Brief Counseling with RET*. Philadelphia, PA: Westminster Press.

Hauck, P. (1982) *How to Do Want You Want to Do*. London: Sheldon.

Higgins, G. O. (1994) *Resilient Adults: Overcoming a Cruel Past*. San Francisco, CA: Jossey-Bass.

Kazantzis, N., Deane, F. P., Ronan, K. R. and L'Abate, L. (2005) *Using Homework Assignments in Cognitive Behavior Therapy*. New York: Routledge.

Kennerley, H., Kirk, J. and Westbrook, D. (2017) *An Introduction to Cognitive Behaviour Therapy: Skills and Applications*, 3rd edn. London: Sage.

Knaus, W. (2002) *The Procrastination Workbook*. Oakland, CA: New Harbinger.

Landsberg, M. (2015) *Mastering Coaching: Practical Insights for Developing High Performance*. London: Profile.

Leahy, R. L. (2005) *The Worry Cure: Stop Worrying and Start Living*. New York: Harmony.

Leahy, R. L. (2017) *Cognitive Therapy Techniques: A Practitioner's Guide*, 2nd edn. New York: Guilford.

Ledley, D. R., Marx, B. P. and Heimberg, R. G. (2010) *Making Cognitive-Behavioral Therapy Work: Clinical Process for New Practitioners*, 2nd edn. New York: Guilford.

Magee, B. (2016) *Ultimate Questions*. Princeton, NJ: Princeton University Press.

Masten, A. S. and Wright, M. O'D. (2010) Resilience over the lifespan: developmental perspectives on resistance, recovery, and transformation, in J. W. Reich, A. J. Zautra and J. S. Hall (eds) *Handbook of Adult Resilience*. New York: Guilford.

Miller, W. R. and Rollnick, S. (2013) *Motivational Interviewing: Helping People Change*, 3rd edn. New York: Guilford.

Mooney, K. A. and Padesky, C. A. (2000) Applying client creativity to recurrent problems: constructing possibilities and tolerating doubt, *Journal of Cognitive Psychotherapy*, 14 (2): 149–161.

Naugle, A. E. and Follette, W. C. (1998) A functional analysis of trauma symptoms, in V. M. Follette, J. I. Ruzek and F. R. Abueg (eds) *Cognitive-Behavioral Therapies for Trauma*. New York: Guilford.

Neenan, M. (2018) *Developing Resilience: A Cognitive-Behavioural Approach*, 2nd edn. Abingdon: Routledge.

Neenan, M. and Dryden, W. (2014) *Life Coaching: A Cognitive Behavioural Approach*, 2nd edn. Hove: Routledge.

Neenan, M. and Palmer, S. (eds) (2012) *Cognitive Behavioural Coaching in Practice: An Evidence Based Approach*. Hove: Routledge.

Nezu, A. M., Nezu, C. M. and D'Zurilla, T. J. (2007) *Solving Life's Problems: A 5-Step Guide to Enhanced Well-Being*. New York: Springer.

Norcross, J. C. (ed.) (2002) *Psychotherapy Relationships That Work: Therapist Contributions and Responsiveness to Patient Needs*. New York: Oxford University Press.

Padesky, C. A. and Greenberger, D. (1995) *Clinician's Guide to Mind Over Mood*. New York: Guilford.

Palmer, S. and Szymanska, K. (2007) Cognitive behavioural coaching: an integrative approach, in S. Palmer and A. Whybrow (eds) *Handbook of Coaching Psychology: A Guide for Practitioners*. Hove: Routledge.

Palmer, S. and Whybrow, A. (2007) Coaching psychology: an introduction, in S. Palmer and A. Whybrow (eds) *Handbook of Coaching Psychology: A Guide for Practitioners*. Hove: Routledge.

Persaud, R. (2001) *Staying Sane: How to Make Your Mind Work for You*. London: Bantam.

Robertson, D. (2010) *The Philosophy of Cognitive-Behavioural Therapy (CBT): Stoic Philosophy as Rational and Cognitive Psychotherapy*. London: Karnac.

Reivich, K. and Shatté, A. (2002) *The Resilience Factor: 7 Keys to Finding Your Inner Strength and Overcoming Life's Hurdles*. New York: Broadway Books.

Safran, J. D. and Muran, J. C. (2000) *Negotiating the Therapeutic Alliance*. New York: Guilford.

Scott, M. J. (2009) *Simply Effective Cognitive Behaviour Therapy*. Hove: Routledge.

Sperry, L. (2004) *Executive Coaching: The Essential Guide for Mental Health Professionals*. Hove: Brunner-Routledge.

Stanier, M. B. (2016) *The Coaching Habit: Say Less, Ask More and Change the Way You Lead Forever*. Toronto, ON: Box of Crayons Press.

Tompkins, M. A. (2004) *Using Homework in Psychotherapy*. New York: Guilford.

Treadway, M. T. (2015) Neural mechanisms of maladaptive schemas and modes in personality disorders, in A. T. Beck, D. D. Davis and A. Freeman (eds) *Cognitive Therapy of Personality Disorders*, 3rd edn. New York: Guilford.

Warburton, N. (2007) *Thinking from A to Z*, 3rd edn. Abingdon: Routledge.

Weishaar, M. E. (1996) Developments in cognitive therapy, in W. Dryden (ed.) *Developments in Cognitive Therapy: Historical Perspectives*. London: Sage.

Weisharr, M. E. and Beck, A. T. (1986) Cognitive therapy, in W. Dryden and W. Golden (eds) *Cognitive-Behavioural Approaches to Psychotherapy*. London: Harper and Row.

Williams, M. and Penman, D. (2011) *Mindfulness: A Practical Guide to Finding Peace in a Frantic World*. London: Piatkus.

Index